EAST SIDE STORIES Gang Life in East LA

The morning after a rival gang tried to shoot Chivo for the fourth time. Chivo teaches his daughter how to hold a .32-caliber pistol. Her mother looks on. Boyle Heights

East Side

 powerHouse Books, New York

Stories

Gang Life in East LA

PHOTOGRAPHS *by* Joseph Rodríguez

Essay by Rubén Martínez *Interview with* Luis J. Rodríguez

I wish to thank the following people for making this work possible and helping me along the way:

Bobby Lavender, Community Youth Gang Services; Brother Modesto, Gloria Terrazone, Manuel Garcia, and Sister Inez of Soledad Enrichment Action Center; Father Greg Boyle; Barrio Evergreen, Marianna Maravilla, Eastside Bishops, Latin Kings, Al Capone, Florencia 13, Insane Juvenile Queens, Happy Valley, and Varrio Nuevo Estrada; John Hope Continuation High School; Gilbert Sanchez, Edmund G. "Pat" Brown Institute of Public Affairs; David Newman, Fred C. Nelles California Youth Authority; Benjamin Chapnick, Anh Stack, and Howard Chapnick of Black Star Photo Agency; Konstnarsnamden; The Fund for Investigative Journalism; Alicia Patterson Fellowship; Mother Jones Documentary Fund; Roman Cisneros, Dean of Students, Lincoln High School; Sandy Close, Richard Rodriguez, and Lisa Margonelli of Pacific News Service; Willis Hartshorn, Charles Stainback, David Zaza, and Robert Blake of the International Center of Photography; Brian Young, Phototechnica; Rubén Martínez; and Jose Pallares.

A warm thanks to Paula Curtz for her insight and guidance in helping me with this project. I also wish to thank Yuko Uchikawa of Makers' Studio for the patience and hard work she devoted to the book design; and Daniel Power of powerHouse Books for making this book possible.

I would like to pay homage to
Lil' Oscar, Gyro, Husky, Diablo, Bobby Lavender, Kemo, Pony, and
all those who have been taken away from us.

There are many others who I would like to thank,
especially all those families who let me into their lives
—with much respect!

Joseph Rodríguez
January, 1998

To Zahava

East Side Stories:
Joseph Rodríguez's Images of East L.A.

By Rubén Martínez

AIDA

It is a beautiful house, Aida Quiles's house. An old two-story woodframe with an ample, green front yard. In the living room a twenty-foot-high ceiling dwarfs the oversize red velvet chairs and couches. A grand staircase with oak balustrade leads to the upstairs bedrooms.

The house stands at the end of a long row of aging stuccos and woodframes, just where Arizona Street slams on its brakes and becomes the Pomona Freeway. The fifteen-foot-high sound barrier does not silence the consistent roar of cars shuttling white-collar commuters east and west, between the bedroom communities of the San Gabriel Valley and the high-rise offices in downtown Los Angeles. It is the constant hollow soundtrack to the Quiles's lives.

The house also stands in the heart of Marianna Maravilla territory; Marianna is one of the several cliques of Maravilla, one of the largest and oldest of the Eastside gangs.

Aida Quiles, in her late fifties, mother of ten, sits by the tall dining room windows that look out onto Arizona Street. A warm wind has blown the smog away today and the light from a big, cloudless sky casts a blue glow over her face. She keeps glancing nervously into the blue, toward the birdcage in the front yard where her cockatoos chirp and jump. Another cage in the backyard holds eight white doves. In the living room, there's an aquarium with little turtles. Aida is not really looking at the cockatoos, but to the street beyond, as if watching for an expected but unwelcome visitor.

"I didn't sleep at all last night," she confides.

She is worried about her sons, Ramiro, 17, who is locked up in the California Youth Authority and Daniel, 18, who is in state prison. She is worried about the fallout from the birthday party last weekend for her daughter María, just turned 16. "It was going to be a clean party, no drinking, nothing," she says, but the Los Angeles County Sheriff's Department showed up before the deejay could spin the first record, acting on a tip that weapons were stashed in the house. They found an automatic on the roof by one of the bedroom windows.

She is worried about her eldest son, Joaquín, who was shot at a few days later by some members from Little Valley gang, which claims the territory next to Marianna's. They jumped over the fence behind the garage as he was getting into his dusty Lincoln Mark IV and began firing. Joaquín started the engine and floored it, backing out of the driveway. Aida points to three bullet holes, one on the driver's side of the windshield.

Last night the Little Valley boys jumped over the fence again, fired a couple of rounds at the house, then disappeared into the darkness. Marianna homeboys from all over the 'hood responded, guarding the house all night long, weapons at the ready.

It's life in a war zone. But in the midst of it all, the Quiles family is still that—a family. Yes, the father walked out seven years ago. But Aida remains, at the absolute center of her family, doing everything she can to keep her kids from becoming homicide statistics. In good Mexican Spanish, Aida is *aguantadora*. Enduring, proud of how much abuse she can take and still stand. *Pleitona*. Always ready for a fight, willing to defend the family at all costs— especially when one of her children is involved (even with her own kids, if she feels they've betrayed her trust). *Cariñosa*. Tender, on those long nights the kids come home drunk or bloodied or scared out of their wits because they had a close call in some alley where one moment everything is *tranquilo*, the homeboys just kickin' it with their cans of Bud and maybe a little weed, someone's car stereo sending an oldies tune straight into the soft nostalgic part of their souls, and then the car with headlights off careening out of nowhere and the sudden, terrible flash of an automatic and the bodies diving into the dirt…

She loves them unconditionally, no matter what they do when they walk out the door and into their "other family," Marianna. Because they are her children.

Although this neighborhood is part of what is popularly known as "East L.A.," it actually lies a couple of miles east of the Los Angeles City limit, in what is known, for political and demographic purposes, as "unincorporated Los Angeles County." No city council, no mayor. There is a County Supervisor, a progressive Latina named Gloria Molina, but she represents more than two million people in a district that extends from the L.A. River halfway to the San Gabriel mountains—about thirty miles as the crow flies. Of course, there is a congressional representative and a senator. But Aida Quiles doesn't know their names, has never written them a letter, never voted in an election because she never registered. She does not speak English, though she understands it well enough after almost twenty years of her children talking back to her in that foreign tongue.

Aida Quiles and her family live here; she can barely imagine an escape, other than the succor she provides within the walls of her house, and now even her house is under attack. The irony is, of course, that the rest of America feels under attack too—from people just like Aida Quiles and her sons: immigrants and gang-bangers invading mainstream America.

When Aida first arrived in Los Angeles from Mexico, she packaged sandwiches at a place called John's Catering downtown on Santa Fe Avenue. She held the job for fifteen years. "I slept three hours a night," she recalls. She'd get home in the wee hours at the end of her shift, and be up again at six to get the kids ready for school.

Ramiro and Daniel went through elementary school like typical kids. She was mindful of the risks of the neighborhood, but in an innocent way. "I was always calling them in off the street in the evening." She'd ask them where they'd been; their answer was always, "With friends." She'd implore them not to "pick up bad habits." One day a neighbor told her that Daniel—he was 12, maybe 13—was a full-fledged Marianna member. She didn't believe it. At home he was sweet as always, did what he was told. But then she saw the tattoo on his leg: "MMV," for Marianna Maravilla. Ramiro soon followed, a tattoo scrawled across his stomach. She found it harder to keep them at home. Daniel even began talking back to her. She was losing them to the street.

So she took to defending them on the street. Like the time one of the Marianna homeboys held up a restaurant a few blocks

away, a foolish act—a $10 stickup. The restaurant owner, gun in hand, chased the kid straight down Arizona towards Aida's house, where her sons and several other homeboys were passing the time leaning against their cars. To block the chase, the group formed a human chain—including one, a paraplegic in a wheelchair—while the robber got away.

A squad car pulled up with a screech. Several sheriff's deputies moved to take Ramiro in for the robbery. His sister María yelled, "Why don't you take him?" pointing at the gun-toting restauran-teur. The deputies handcuffed her and moved in on Ramiro, guns drawn. Aida stepped in between, giving Ramiro the split second he needed to escape. One of the deputies grabbed her by the arm and as she pulled away, he lost his balance and fell, prompting laughter all around. Red-faced, he finally restrained Aida, handcuffed her, and threw her into the squad car next to María.

By this time, there was a helicopter circling above. The K-9 unit was brought in; police announced that a dog search for a dangerous criminal was underway and warned everyone to stay indoors.

Aida was beside herself. They could shoot Ramiro. The dogs could tear him to shreds. Since he was on probation, she knew that if they arrested him for suspicion of the robbery or resisting arrest, it would probably mean a prison sentence.

But the sheriffs never found Ramiro. He hid under a car in the driveway next door as the dogs sniffed and the helicopter threw its light into bushes and alleys. A neighbor finally snuck him into her house until the commotion died down. At the station, deputy after deputy tried to take Aida's fingerprints but they couldn't

get a clean image; when they placed her in the holding tank, the door wouldn't stay shut. Aida and María were released without any charges.

"It was a night of miracles," she says.

But now, most days, Aida is virtually a prisoner in her own home. She won't summon the prison guards—the Sheriff's Department—for help; her experience shows they can do more harm than good. Even trying to keep the kids in school seems questionable: classrooms in East L.A. are rife with gangs. School can be as dangerous as the streets.

Why doesn't she just move to another neighborhood? She had a reason from the day she moved in—someone tossed a Molotov cocktail into a car parked in front of the house the first night she spent on Arizona Street—but she genuinely thought things would get better. Later, moving was out of the question: another neighborhood would mean the kids would have to face rival gangmembers. Did she overestimate what she could provide for her children at home? Did she underestimate the allure of the street?

She's scared to leave the house for even a few hours. She used to spend a lot of time away from home: she played bingo obsessively for a couple of years; her collection of little Buddhas and gold elephants sitting in the china cabinet are good luck charms to beat the odds. But her children got into more and more trouble while she was away. Daniel started using drugs; God knows what else he and Ramiro were up to with the homeboys. Now she won't even go to parties or out dancing. And no more bingo. "Not even if I was assured of winning a million dollars."

Perhaps Aida has become a kind of gangmember herself. She's barricaded in her "territory," constantly on the watch for her sons' rivals, who are no longer just other barrio children to her, but threats to the survival of her family. She even welcomes the Marianna homeboys and their weapons: better that they kill defending her family than one of her own getting killed. She sounds more guilty about playing bingo than about the automatic the sheriffs found on the roof.

Aida still believes that warmth and love at home can be the salve for the wounding world outside. It is a deeply held Mexican belief: the family is the hub of life, and the mother is at the center. But Mexicans never expected an inner-city nightmare when they crossed the border. Ill-prepared for a culture of youth violence unknown back home (gangs are exported to Mexico, not the other way around) and lacking political know-how in a system that is stacked against them, the Quileses remain trapped between an Old World memory and an unreachable American future.

Aida Quiles has a beautiful house. But it might not be enough to save her kids.

THE GANGSTER

The myth of the Outsider—the outlaw—is virtually as old as America, a cherished part of our folklore. In its early incarnations, it spoke to the country's sense of itself as a band of misfits on a quest for liberty. The pilgrims were religious or criminal outlaws. Depending on your perspective, early arrivals were Freedom Fighters or dangerous zealots, visionaries or evil incarnate. They were Americans.

Thus Billy the Kid—by all accounts a ruthless killer—still goes down in our cultural history as an American hero. The only prerequisite for such anointment is some sense that the outlaws had themselves been victims before they turned violent. Among the gunslingers of the Old West were Confederate soldiers who had faced devastation in the South. And in the 1920s and 1930s, Americans could project their frustrations over Prohibition and the Depression onto gangsters of the day. So while Bonnie and Clyde killed innocent bank clerks, they became heroine and hero to many in the soup lines who considered the crimes of big capital against working people at least as egregious as the gang's.

But today's street kids, Aida's sons and tens of thousands of others like them in the inner cities of America—Latino "cholos" and black "gangsta's" (black and brown both use the term "homeboy," a noun sanctifying the only place they can call "home," their gang's own territory)—aren't heroes to anyone, perhaps not even to themselves. In fact, blacks and Mexicans never qualified for that status, even though they were authentic Outsiders in every way. Mexicans who turned to a life of crime in the Southwest after the Mexican-American War were never considered outlaws in the heroic sense. The gringos called them "bandidos," emphasizing ethnic otherness and conjuring an image of darkness and depravity. To Anglo Californians of the late 1800s, Joaquín Murietta—a legendary bandit-rebel—was a cold-blooded killer. But to Mexican-American Californians, he represented a virtual one-man insurrection against the gringos who had stolen their lands and dignity.

A few literary and cinematic portrayals in the late nineteenth and early twentieth centuries—the dashing "Spanish" romance of

Ramona, The Cisco Kid, Zorro, etc.—did little to clean up the lingering bandido image. From the "greaser" character in *The Treasure of the Sierra Madre* who snarled at Bogart about "steenking badges" to today's typical images of Chicanos as gangbangers, drug runners, lusty señoritas or matronly-types-with-many-babies, Hollywood carries 150-year-old cultural baggage in its representation of Mexican-Americans: Americans have never seen "Mexicans" as "Americans." They are always the Other, to be lusted after or feared.

The Evergreen gang featured in this book calls the Boyle Heights District home, within the city limit, unlike Marianna, a few miles east, but both are part of greater East L.A., also known as the Eastside, one of the country's biggest and most mythologized barrios. East L.A. constantly vies with Spanish Harlem in the American pop imagination as stereotype of the Latin. Lowrider Chevrolets bouncing up and down on their hydraulic lifts. *Cholas* with foot-high bouffants and heavy mascara, Zoot Suiters with their outrageous "drapes," Mexican simpleton characters. These images are rooted in fragments of reality, of course, as are most stereotypes, but we laugh at these, as we do with many things we can't understand. The laughter is a product of the social distance between "us" and "them."

THE EASTSIDE STORY

Prior to World War I, Boyle Heights and parts of unincorporated Los Angeles to the east of the city were relatively affluent areas; there are still a few elegant Victorians dotting the landscape. In the 1920s, cheaper housing and immigration made of East L.A. a California version of New York's Lower East Side: Jews, Italians, Armenians, Japanese. East L.A.'s main commercial thoroughfare was even named "Brooklyn" in a nostalgic nod to the East Coast origins of many of the immigrants. (Recently the name was changed to "César Chávez," in honor of the late Chicano farmworker leader, but except for young Chicano radicals, most people still refer to it as "la Bru-kleen.")

At about the same time, the Mexican Revolution (1910-17) sent the first twentieth-century wave of Mexican immigrants to California. The early barrio was a ramshackle collection of houses and shacks in and around the historic center of the original Mexican pueblo at Olvera Street. (To this day, thousands of

Mexicans and Chicanos are drawn by a race-memory magnet every Sunday to La Placita, the old pueblo church there.) Conditions ranged from livable to squalid, but, with the continuing flood of refugees, quickly grew unbearably dense, pushing those who were to become the pioneers of the Mexican barrio of East L.A. towards Boyle Heights.

From the beginning, the immigrant Mexicans were on their own in their new (though historically speaking old) home. Then as now, they did not come looking for welfare handouts—most first-generation Mexicans are too proud to even entertain the thought of any charity—but for work. There was plenty to be had. Agribusiness flourished throughout Los Angeles and Orange Counties; tens of thousands of Mexicans picked the orange groves of the San Fernando Valley. Brickyards, garment factories and, later, the automobile industry (General Motors, Firestone, Goodyear) were also stocked with Mexican labor.

Politically speaking, the Mexicans were on their own too, isolated from the Anglo power brokers at City Hall. And so they developed, like other groups of immigrants and refugees, "*mutualistas,*" mutual aid societies. Ties with Mexico remained strong. Revolutionaries like the Flores Magón brothers organized exile cadres in Los Angeles and other towns closer to the border for quixotic missions back home, did fundraising, promised a new Mexico for the refugees to return to.

But the new Mexico never really materialized, especially not in the impoverished lands of the northern and central provinces, where most of the refugees came from. And so what was to have been a temporary stay became permanent. The barrio continued to grow, and began its transformation into a "Mexican-American" community. By the 1940s, most of the European immigrants had moved on to the greener pastures of the booming San Fernando Valley and the Westside of Los Angeles. East L.A. came to be known as the "Mexican part of town," and was literally the other side of the tracks: the "height" in Boyle Heights is a gentle rise of land immediately east of the Santa Fe Railroad and the L.A. River.

Mexicans were not to go through the same rite of passage to Americanization as other immigrant groups: scapegoats for the Great Depression in California, they were sent back to Mexico by the hundreds of thousands in the Repatriation of the 1930s.

And despite the fact that they were invited back to the picking fields and the factories for the war effort, and despite the fact that Mexican-Americans by the thousands signed up and were sent overseas (and won more medals proportionate to their number in the armed forces than any other group), at home they were still foreigners. Public swimming pools displayed signs announcing "Wednesdays for Mexicans Only." Schools were de-facto segregated. And the pachucos, the first urban Mexican-American gangs, quickly became the favorite whipping boys of local politicians and law enforcement.

The first pachuco cliques formed in East Los Angeles in the late 1920s and 1930s. By today's standards, they were innocent—fights were usually waged with fists, occasionally with knives and chains—and they resembled street toughs more than today's gang-members. Aesthetics were all-important. The highstyle of the Zoot Suit (pants up near the breastbone, chain and fob swinging down below the knee) was an exaggeration, a subversion of typical American fashion. Like the lowrider cars of the sixties and seventies, the Zoot Suit wasn't meant to be worn so much as seen (although it had its functional side, too: loose clothes were perfect for the acrobatics of Chicano swing dancing, just as today's "baggies" allow for hip hop). It was a badge of cultural rebellion, and the virtual birth of Chicano culture: to Americans, the Zoot Suiters still looked Mexican; to Mexicans in the Old Country, they looked far too gringo.

The pachucos were seen as foreigners—despite the fact that their older brothers or dads and uncles were in the service—and easy targets for war-time xenophobia. The so-called Zoot Suit Riots of 1942 did not start, as the jingoistic *Los Angeles Times* of the era reported, with crazed Chicano youths attacking Anglo servicemen. Rather, off-duty sailors went on hunting expeditions, stripping and beating any "hoodlum" unlucky enough to be caught on the street wearing his "drapes."

The social walls around the barrio grew higher and higher. Consider historian Carey McWilliams's description of Chicano nightlife in 1940s Los Angeles:

> While the fancier 'palladiums' have known to refuse [the pachucos], even when they have had the price of admission, there are other dance halls, not nearly so fancy, that make a business of catering to their needs. It should be noted, however, that Mexican boys never willingly accepted these inferior accommodations and the inferior status they connote. Before they have visited the 'joints' on Skid Row, they have first tried to pass through palatial foyers on Sunset Boulevard. When they finally give up, they have few illusions left about their native land.

McWilliams, one of California's premier historians, served as chairman of the Sleepy Lagoon Defense Committee in the early 1940s, formed after an entire "gang" of Chicano youths was rounded up and convicted of murder in a trial that made a mockery of American jurisprudence—including an "expert" witness who testified that the Mexican "race" was predisposed to barbaric behavior because of its savage Indian ancestry (testimony that remained on the record). The enmity between law enforcement and Chicano youth thus dates back at least half a century.

This is heavily documented history. Two blue-ribbon panels (the McCone Commission which investigated the causes of the Watts Riots of 1965 and the Christopher Commission which looked into the Rodney King incident in 1991) found that Mexicans or blacks participating in no obvious criminal activity are regularly taught a lesson by the LAPD—whether they're hardcore gang-members or innocent party-crew types. Their cars are pulled over for purely harassment purposes. They are ordered to "assume the position," kneeling with hands locked behind their heads.

The result is a severely limited world—a world hemmed in by fear. Fear of the police, of "white" society, of the entire world beyond the L.A. River. "I thought that Soto Street to Atlantic Boulevard to the Sears building was the whole world," says Joey Pallares, a youth counselor at Wilson High School who grew up on the Eastside. "I thought everyone was brown, that just teachers and doctors were white. I'd never even been to the beach."

With the 1960s came heightened awareness of the barrio's social and economic isolation. César Chávez and the United Farm Workers marched and fasted, high school students across the Eastside staged the famous "blowouts," walking out of classes to demand more resources for barrio schools.

But the Chicano Movement itself highlighted old wounds over identity. Integrationists battled separatists: are we Mexican, or American, or Mexican-American? From the time of the Mexican Revolution to the passage in 1994 of Proposition 187 (which seeks to deny public education and health benefits to undocumented—i.e., mostly Mexican—immigrants), generation after generation of Mexican youth has faced essentially the same quandary. Unlike the other immigrants—the Jews and Poles, the Italians and Irish—who arrived at roughly the same time, the Mexicans of the Eastside are still not considered Americans. Proposition 187 recalls the Repatriation of the 1930s. The cops still harass the kids. Barrio schools are still inferior. Chicanos are still trapped between Old World ideals of family and solidarity and American notions of individual ambition and upward mobilty.

Inner-city violence appears to have grown as the sense of isolation and frustration deepens. Fistfights evolved into knife-fights, followed by Old West-like gun duels, and, finally, drive-by shootings. There are myriad explanations offered for the escalation: increased Mexican gang involvement in the drug trade; easier access to guns; the failure of the civil rights movement (and liberal/ethnic politics) to fundamentally transform inner-city life; the overall society's drift toward a culture of violence. One cause stands out: the collapse in the 1980s of Southern California's aerospace and automobile industries, once the primary source of upwardly mobile, union-scale jobs for those in the barrio.

With nowhere to go, the barrio turns inward. The neighbor-hood becomes the world, and families carry the weight of that world. The Mexican culture's reliance on intimacy in the private realm (the Catholic version of WASP "family values") appears to help set the stage for both heroic and tragic events in the barrio. Families like Aida's—fatherless households, not uncommon even in Mexico—manage to survive with a sense of "us against the world," the world being the sheriff's department, rival gangmembers, bill collectors.

There are indications that even this most sacred of Mexican institutions is beginning to break apart. UCLA public health professor David Hayes-Bautista has noted that the healthiest barrio families are those that maintain their Mexican traditions—in diet, in child-rearing, in cultural rituals, etc. Children of first-generation immigrants are less prone to illness, injury, and death by violence than those of the second and third generation. In other words, Hayes-Bautista says, American culture may be bad for the barrio's health.

As hope recedes, the barrio family continues to retreat into itself. It also works to repair itself: if the nuclear unit disintegrates, the extended family plays a crucial role: an aunt or uncle steps in if mother or father are gone; cousins can become surrogate siblings; grandparents often live with their children and their adult children's children. This notion of blood solidarity has probably saved more kids from the streets than all the "outreach" efforts combined, even before such programs were severely cut back in the late eighties.

At the same time, there are traits at the heart of the Mexican family that may be intimately related to gang violence. Do barrio mothers sometimes inadvertently reinforce their sons' violent behavior through a not-so-secret admiration of their exaggerated male bravado (a macho rebel onto which mothers can project their own frustrations)? Does the "intimacy" of the family become suf-focating, as some sociologists have conjectured, and inhibit passage from adolescent rebellion to an adult sense of responsibility?

What is clear is that gangs proliferate in the barrio and in the 'hood as a response to public and private failure. The gang is the "family" of last resort: a family for kids when the parents are absent, abusive, or just worn down by the pressures of barrio life; a school when public education disintegrates; a culture unto itself when neither side of the U.S.-Mexican border seems to provide any sense of rootedness.

The vast majority of gang violence is internecine. The rage turns inward: the gang kid blows away his mirror image, another gang kid. Thus every drive-by shooting is nothing less than ethnic suicide, a bloodletting between brothers (and, increasingly, sisters). A good part of the war on the streets of the Eastside—with all its roots in politics, in economics, in a history of racism and self-negation—will likely be won or lost within the heart of the barrio family.

For countless gang and non-gang kids in the barrio, there is someone like Aida Quiles trying anything and everything to save them from the streets. The problem for the rest of us is that when we see the barrio—and we see it only through the media and Hollywood—we only see the victims and perpetrators of the violence. In the American imagination, Aida doesn't exist.

THE MENACE, THE MYTH

Now and again, a gang member commits a crime outside the barrio upon an innocent bystander of another ethnicity and social status. Such incidents bring out politicians and editorial writers who call for military-style police sweeps to root out the "thugs," or, in more recent lexicon, urban "terrorists."

They are known as anything but children.

But of course that's what they are. Children who sometimes commit monstrous crimes. If we take a closer look at the tragedy, the lines between victim and victimizer can blur. "Who dies first? The one who catches the bullet or the one who pulls the trigger?" asks Father Greg Boyle, the Jesuit priest whose gang ministry in Boyle Heights has won national acclaim as well as repudiation for its "unconditional love" approach to gang youth. "There is no shortage of heartache here. Victim and victimizer alike call us to compassion." Boyle has a simple message: no one is beyond redemption. According to Boyle, redemption can be as simple a matter as finding a decent job.

It is simple to view the barrio from afar with revulsion, or pity, or both. But the distance emphasizes our complicity. Macho conservatives raise the flag of self-reliance and individual will—a refrain espoused by Louis Farrakhan as well as Bob Dole—as the ultimate antidote for the violence of the inner city. Liberals still hold the greater society responsible for the tragedy, their patronizing hearts bleeding for the ghetto dwellers. But doesn't the individual will of the barrio youth have to be matched by the society's acceptance of that youth through the end of all forms of discrimination? If there has been a failure of will in the barrio, it has been matched by a failure of society to entertain any solutions other than gang sweeps and prison-building. The solution to inner-city violence lies both in the barrio and in the suburb, in the private and public realms.

The irony is that while the social gap between the suburb and the barrio rapidly expands in cities like Los Angeles, there is an actual diminishing of physical distance between the two. The San Fernando Valley, once one huge, white, middle-class bedroom community, is increasingly Mexican, Central American, and working class. The affluent "gated communities"—the fortresses of the Valley, akin to "Off World," the levitating suburbia prophesied in *Bladerunner*, Ridley Scott's apocalyptic classic on L.A.—are now only blocks away from apartment buildings teeming with Chicanos and new immigrants from Mexico, Central America, and Asia.

However, political power is still concentrated in the white, middle-class enclaves and that determines, to a great extent, the conditions of life in the inner city. Measures like California's "Three Strikes You're Out" law, mandating a life prison sentence after a third felony conviction, and Proposition 187 are being emulated nationwide.

And yet there is a kind of dialogue going on, not on the level of politics or economics, but culturally. Black rap is more popular with white suburban teens than with black kids; the vapid culture of the suburb leads them to desire their inner-city other. Middle-class kids talk the talk (black), wear baggies and Pendleton shirts (Chicano), turn their baseball caps backward, play out gangsta' fantasies. And the kids of the barrio or the 'hood act out suburban fantasies by imitating middle-class affluence with fancy cars, gold chains, and brand name shoes. The 'burb kid and the inner-city *cholo* or gangsta' share the same existential void, and both fill it with the same violent aesthetic. Rap's glorification of killing rival gangmembers or cops is the selfsame "mainstream" adulation of Stallone and Segall blowing away the "bad guys," who just happen to be mostly non-white. The difference is, of course, that life in the suburbs is a video game, while in the inner city, it often plays out with mortal consequences. *But it is the same culture.*

Nowhere is the distance between suburb and inner city, rich and poor, white and non-white, more obvious than in the mass media's portrayal of gang violence. Newspaper headlines and images on the nightly news show us that we are at war. There is no relief from the constant stream of violent imagery: the prone body lying in a pool of blood behind the yellow police tape; LAPD officers handcuffing young men lying face down on the pavement; defiant homeboys mugging for the cameras, flashing gang signs. "Special Reports" apprise us of the latest pathologies of the inner city and add to our anxiety. The story of Stephanie Kuhen is a prime example.

On the night of September 18, 1995, Stephanie Kuhen, age 3, was riding in a car with her 2-year-old brother, her mother, and uncle in the Cypress Park area of Los Angeles—a mostly Latino barrio. A family friend, Timothy Stone, who was driving the car, made a wrong turn into a dead-end alley as he was looking for a short-cut home. A crew of homeboys surrounded the car, and, while Stone was trying to make his way back out, opened fire.

Stephanie was struck in the head by a bullet and killed; Stone and Stephanie's brother were wounded.

The story made immediate national headlines. The *Los Angeles Times*, in its first account of the incident, called Stephanie's death a "classic urban nightmare." In the days that followed, we learned that the kids in the alley—several of the suspects were under 18 years of age—were members of the Avenues gang, an old clique in the Highland Park area of Los Angeles. Countless news reports opened with the image or description of the graffiti-scarred entrance to the alley, which featured the sinister message, *"Avenida asecinos"* (Avenue of the Assassins, in misspelled Spanish). The cumulative impact of the coverage was the impression that any gangmember in Los Angeles was capable of gunning down a 3-year-old in cold blood.

The *L.A. Times* published at least seventy-two stories that focused on or mentioned Stephanie's death. But critics pointed out that several other recent incidents in which the murdered child had been black or Latino had not received the same level of press coverage. The inescapable conclusion is that the media treated Stephanie's death differently because she was white.

Indeed, in the months following her death, the *L.A. Times* published two stories about other children gunned down in similar circumstances: Erika Izquierdo, an 11-year-old Latina from Huntington Park, and Victor Neal, an 8-year-old African American boy from Compton. There were no follow-up stories on either incident. Meanwhile, the story of a questionable officer-involved shooting of a 14-year-old Latino boy in the Eastside neighborhood of Lincoln Heights, which led to two days of rioting, was featured or mentioned in only seven separate articles.

A "news analysis" piece in the *L.A. Times* a few weeks after Stephanie's death denied that race was the driving factor behind the paper's treatment of the story. One expert even implied that Stephanie was somehow more innocent than other children killed in the barrio:

> In most cases, victims come under scrutiny; they do not instantly garner sympathy just because they were murdered. Everyone weighs a crime story trying to determine if the victim, in some way, brought the crime upon himself. City dwellers have become hardened to urban crimes, such as gang- or drug-related deaths. . .
> In those, there seems to be provocation and a sense that the victim contributed to his demise.

Did 11-year-old Erika and 8-year-old Victor, simply by living in the ghetto, contribute to their deaths?

The biggest distortion of the Stephanie Kuhen story was the description of her tragic death as a "classic urban nightmare." The Kuhen story, in reality, was a classic suburban nightmare: the image of a white family making a wrong turn into a black or brown ghetto and paying the ultimate price. The irony is that the Kuhens don't fit the stereotype of the white middle-class family. A little reported fact is that the family lived very close to the "Avenue of the Assassins," and that, by most standards, they were a lower middle- to working-class family living virtually next door to a Latino barrio.

The point here is not to deny the obvious. There is indeed a great amount of violence in the barrio and in the 'hood; what should be equally obvious is that not every black or Latino youngster is a gangmember, not every gangmember is a murderer.

Most are not. Just because a kid is wearing baggies, an oversize white T-shirt and has a crewcut does not mean that he's packing a .38 Special in his waistband—he could be a party-crew member, a simple "tagger," or a graffiti artist who eschews violence.

But this book is not concerned so much with most of the kids in the barrio. It is an unflinching look at the "bad" kids—the very ones we're obsessed with. Joe Rodríguez's message is that even the most vicious killer-kid (and there are some in this book) *is still our kid.* This book is not the "mothers of assassins still love their sons" cliché. Rather, it is the moral challenge of never giving up on the possibility of redemption, of honestly looking at what we ourselves could have done to avoid the tragedy, and of wondering what, if any, responsibility we share in it.

HUSKY

In memory of 'Husky' beloved friend and homeboy Dec. 20,1975-Sep. 7,1993. Para nuestro querido hijo, nieto, sobrino y primo, que descanses en paz y en nuestros corazones siempre vivirás. [For our beloved son, grandson, nephew and cousin, may you rest in peace and in our hearts forever live.]

His photograph on the plaque, next to the epitaph, is grainy, out of focus. Husky looks anything but a vicious Evergreen gang-member: plain white T-shirt, unsmiling, with his thin, 18-year-old's mustache. He's too young to act so formal.

Marisela Vásquez comes out here to Resurrection Cemetery about once a week. Sometimes she brings a blanket, and falls asleep next to the grave in the late afternoon. "I feel at peace here," she says. "Husky," born Jesús Navarro Vásquez, she explains, is her cousin. Still "is," despite the fact that he died three years ago.

In her late twenties, Marisela wears a sharp office outfit (she works for IBM), and her features are clearly Mexican Indian: round face, black eyes, flattened nose, full lips. The family hails from the state of Jalisco, where she was born. There is much of Jalisco—much of the Mexican Indian—here at Resurrection Cemetery, about five miles east of Evergreen. The clients are nearly all Mexican and Chicano, and their families take good care of them. Nearly every gravesite here has fresh flowers: white lilies, yellow daisies, purple irises. Cellophane balloons, Styrofoam hearts. Just a few paces away from Husky's grave, Marisela shows me "Gyro's" marker and, another few paces away, "Diablo's."

The three teenagers grew up together in the Evergreen neighborhood of Boyle Heights. They died almost within a year of each other, all gunned down on the streets of the Eastside. Diablo himself jumped Husky into Evergreen when Husky was 13. The ritual beating took place among the old tombstones and plaques-with-photographs at Evergreen Cemetery, across the street from Husky's grandmother's house—the place of choice for Evergreen boys to be initiated into the gang. The three were together in life and death. Husky died in Gyro's arms; Diablo and Gyro were there to bury Husky; Diablo attended Gyro's funeral. "Diablo told them, 'Wait for me in Heaven,'" says Marisela. "Now they're all together again."

Husky was Marisela's favorite nephew—a special distinction, considering she has sixteen nieces and nephews in all. "Me and 'Jesse' [her nickname for Husky] were the best of friends," she tells me. "I never realized how much he loved me until he threatened to kill my boyfriend." She explains. Her boyfriend at the time—today her husband—had a temper he couldn't always control. Jesse heard a rumor that he'd hit her. One day she pulled into her driveway and found Jesse sitting on the porch waiting for her.

Seconds later, her boyfriend pulled up in his car. Jesse approached him, and she heard him say: "I don't know what happened, but if you ever touch her again, I'll kill you."

She says it again: "He'd be willing to kill someone for me, that's how much he loved me."

Husky grew up in Evergreen. Like Marianna, it is one of the older gang neighborhoods; the Evergreen gang has been around since the 1950s. He was a nice kid, Marisela says, but "not too smart." Concerned teachers would show up at her house. "They'd come to me, because Jesse would mention his *tía* [aunt] 'Marcie.'" The Anglo science teacher told her: "He talks a lot about you. You should talk to him."

She became his confidante. She'd write him letters and mail them by post just for the fun of it (he lived a couple of blocks away). She counseled him on school and relationships, on the virtue of respect for family and elders. That Husky would mention his *tía* to his teachers and not his own mother speaks to problems at home. Marisela shakes her head about her sister, Husky's mom. There was drinking and fighting in the house, she says. To escape, he'd spend a lot of time at his grandmother's and at Marcie's.

After he was jumped into Evergreen, Husky was kicked out of Stevenson Junior High for fighting, and transferred to Hollenbeck. He stayed around long enough to graduate. Later, he was kicked out of Roosevelt High for fighting and transferred to Lincoln, where he lasted all of one day before facing off with rival gangmembers and getting kicked out of school one last time. But at home, Marcie says, he was still the sensitive, if somewhat troubled, Jesse. "The way he was as a small kid is the way he was when he was 17," she says. "I didn't know the Jesse that walked out that front door. With us he was kind, sweet, had respect for his elders. He was noble."

One day Husky told Marisela, "Why can't we have a family, why can't we be all together?" He was talking about his strained relationship with his parents, the bickering among the rest of the Vásquez clan. "I cried at seeing how bad he felt," she says, and remembers how Husky pinched his nose with his thumb and forefinger, trying to hold back his own tears. "I'm going to get them all together," he told Marisela.

A few days later, Marisela asked Husky to fix a hole in the roof of her building, promising to buy him a double bed as payment for the chore. Early that evening, he told her that he was going out to grab a bite to eat with some friends. "I looked at him as he left, at the back of his head as he walked away," she says. "I had a bad feeling." A few hours later, Marisela's mother, Husky's grandmother, walked into her room with a rosary swinging from trembling hands. She could only summon one word: "Jesse."

"Instead of buying him a bed, I bought him a coffin," says Marisela. "That's a big—what do you call it?—irony."

"But he did what he said he was going to do. He got the family all together again. For his funeral."

THE RAGE

One of Husky's friends knew something about the "other Husky," the one who walked out the door of his family's home into his gang life. "I have the rage inside me, and I've seen it in them. Husky had it in him, too. He wasn't crazy like some other guys, who'll shoot you without thinking twice. But he had some of the rage."

I have seen the rage. At Dolores Mission Church in Boyle Heights once during a special farewell mass for "gang priest" Father Greg Boyle (who was enroute to what ended up being only a temporary assignment away from his parish), a hardcore kid starting picking fights. There were hundreds of people around— grandmothers, tots, celebrities—and there were TV news crews, but it wasn't an act for the cameras. As he flashed gang signs, spewed epithets and shoved, it seemed that he was being driven by some narrow but volcanic part of himself that no one, least of all the kid himself, could control. But the rage was gone, as quickly as it came. Minutes later the homeboy was hugging Father Greg, bidding him well in his new job.

Husky always wanted to get out of the house, his homeboy remembers. "He'd say, 'Let's go to the beach.' He'd say he was tired of hanging out in the neighborhood. He always wanted to go drive around in my car and pick up girls. 'Let's go cruising,' he'd say. 'Let's pick up some chicks, get some beer, and kick back.' "

Many homeboys talk about their desire to the leave the 'hood. Typically, they are vague dreams of leaving "the life" behind for a straight job, a family, and a house in the suburbs. For those who never leave, any short trip out of the barrio—excursions to the beach, Universal Studios, or Tijuana—take on mythical proportions. But the 'hood always pulls back. It is an affair with the famous "Born to Lose" philosophy of the barrio, an extreme form of Catholic fatalism that is terrifyingly powerful as it is elaborate. Everything is ritualized, stylized, kitsch-ified, from the "jumping in" of new gangmembers to the car washes held to raise money to bury fallen homeboys; life and death are more stylized than Disney or Scorcese. But the style often affirms death over life.

Early one evening, some friends stopped by Husky's. On their way to visit their friend Gypsy, they stopped to grab a bite to eat at a taco truck. They were eating off the top of the car when a kid they didn't recognize approached them.

"This is Barrio Stoners," he said. It was true; they'd crossed into Stoners territory. Husky was the first to react: he flashed the Evergreen sign with his hands and said, "You know what? I'm from Evergreen!" The Stoners kid responded, "Fuck Evergreen!" and a second later pulled out a gun and started firing wildly.

Husky turned to dive into the back seat of the car; Gyro jumped into the front to start the engine. The gunman fired virtually pointblank at the back seat: Husky raised his hands against the bullet, a desperate gesture that allowed a bullet to pierce his side, tear through his chest cavity, and sever an artery.

The shooting stopped—maybe the gun was empty, maybe it jammed.

Gyro dragged Husky out of the backseat and helped him run down the middle of the street as cars honked and slammed their brakes, Husky bleeding the whole way. Gyro frantically dialed 911 on payphones as they ran. After two long blocks, Husky collapsed in front of a pizza place. Gyro asked the people inside to call for help; they refused. Finally, at another payphone, he called Gypsy, who arrived in his car within minutes, before police and the ambulance. Gyro held Husky in his arms as the car raced down the street toward Santa Marta hospital. He was pronounced dead shortly after arrival.

Husky's death left deep scars among the Evergreen homeboys. Gyro and Diablo were stunned by their best friend's death. They went through the barrio rituals: the car washes to help pay for the casket and burial, the grieving at the rosary, kissing Husky's cold forehead in the casket, stroking his stiff hand. Both of them distanced themselves from the gang after Husky's death. "Husky's death was a big blow to Gyro," an Evergreen homie tells me. "It kind of opened up his eyes, and he started to fade away from the gang." Marisela Vásquez tells me virtually the same thing about Diablo: "After Jesse passed away, he changed. He was still in the gang, but he was in school and he was doing good."

Gyro was killed at a gas station halfway between Evergreen and Marianna territory. His job at a tire shop started at five in the morning, and he decided to gas the car up the night before. Some younger Evergreen homeboys, itching for a chance to "go for a ride," asked to tag along. A car pulled alongside his while he was pumping gas. The usual "Where you from?" taunt escalated into shouts, and, finally, bullets. Gyro jumped in the car and hauled out of the station, but the car carrying the rival gangmembers followed him, shooting all the way.

One bullet went through the rear window, the driver's side car seat and, finally, through Gyro's back.

Diablo's death occurred under murkier circumstances. He was attending a now-defunct alternative school downtown. The faculty, all dedicated inner-city youth activists each and every one of them, touted the school as a place where gang rivalries and racial tensions were dealt with directly through intensive dialogue and conflict resolution; a place where the style of clothes and colors of skin did not lead to the inevitable. But word in Evergreen has it that Diablo died precisely as a result of tensions with black gangmembers at the school, tensions that turned deadly once the kids were back out on the street.

THE FAMILY

The chapel is a small A-frame building shaded by a few tall eucalyptus trees. It sits on a hill overlooking the hills and valleys of Evergreen. There is a cross at the apex, strung with colored lights that blink every night, a neighborhood beacon. The unpainted cement walls dried imperfectly and formed hairline cracks. Red roses and ferns grow in tin cans along the narrow stoop. Three wooden stairs lead up to a padlocked door.

Nino Vásquez, Husky's uncle, opens the chapel for me, but waits outside as I walk in. It is warm inside compared to the early Sunday morning chill outside, the heat coming from the candles burning at the center of the altar. There are prayers and songs, some written on paper, others on the walls graffiti-style. A flyer announcing a car wash for Gyro's funeral. Another one for Diablo's. And one, of course, for Husky's.

To one side of the altar is Husky's old dresser drawer. His clothes are still inside. His shoes are on the floor, waiting for him to slip them on. An open pack of his favorite cigs, Marlboro reds, lies next to one of the candles. And at the very center of the wall behind the altar, where Christ would be, is a photograph of Husky.

It's a comical picture. He's in a *Playgirl*-like pose, reclining on his bed, one hand behind his head. A chubby, teddy-bear body. Homeboy crew cut, white T-shirt. His face has the same tense, complex look of the photograph on his grave plaque. It looks like he's just kickin' it, but he's not totally relaxed. He seems to be asking a question, afraid of the answer.

Outside, Nino has been joined by Marisela and their nephew Tony, a clean-cut-looking teenager. Nino tells me that Husky had already been shot twice before the third and fatal confrontation. "I visited him in the hospital the first time. The next time, I didn't. I told him later that he was acting like he wanted to die. He said he was going to die anyway. And he said that I would cry upon hearing of his death. And look," he says, wiping tears away, "his prophecy is still being fulfilled today."

Nino Vásquez built the chapel in his backyard with his own hands shortly after Husky's death. He has four children, three sons and a daughter; the oldest 23, the youngest 9. He's worked as a welder to provide for the family. He used to get $11 an hour; now he's getting six, seven. No medical insurance. He feels like his American dream is slipping away.

The altar is both a memorial to Husky and a constant reminder of his own children's vulnerability, a cautionary tale for the family. "I tell my kids not to go out," he says. "My sons tell me they're just going to visit their girlfriends. Only they know where they really go. The thing with this violence is that it really doesn't matter whether they're in the gang or not.

What happened to Jesse could happen just as easily to them, for no reason."

We are slowly joined by more and more of the Vásquez clan. Tony's mom (Nino and Marisela's sister) Ana, with her younger son Paul and her youngest, Stephanie; Nino's sons Saúl and Heriberto, and his daughter, Lily; Husky's younger sister, Rosa; and the family matriarch, Victoriana, a white-haired, crinkle-faced, venerable Mexicana. They step into the chapel alone or two or three at a time, the little ones bouncing about, the older ones quieter.

The memories tumble out. Tony talks the most. He says he comes to the chapel to "kick back here with Jesse, just like we used to." He insists that Husky is still with the family. "You know that little kids can see the dead?" he says. "I wish I was Stephanie's age so that I could see him." Tony idolized—still idolizes—Husky. "He taught me to smoke, to tag [graffiti], to drink, drive a car, jack [steal] a car, jack a stereo, play with guns—" he pauses, perhaps jarred by the realization that he's telling me all this within earshot of his mother, aunt, uncle, and grandmother. "But I don't want to do that." Later, Tony talks about graduating from high school next year

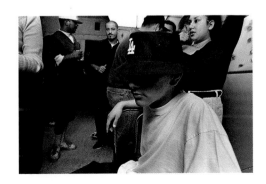

and his dream of attending a trade school in Phoenix, Arizona. He is a very bright kid, and he's clearly and painfully split between emulating Husky's outlaw life and doing right by his family.

"The last time I saw Husky," Tony says, "I told him, 'Take me with you, you fucker.' But he told me, 'You better go to school tomorrow.' He had a sad look, like a 'my time's up' kind of look. I was asleep when the phone rang…"

Victoriana comes out of her taciturn silence and recalls his last meal. "He asked me for bread instead of tortillas, and I told him he was too American," she says. She would plead with him to leave the life. Husky responded simply, honestly: there was no way he could. She told him they'd kill him. And he'd repeat: I can't. "What do they get out of it?" Victoriana wonders. "Do they get paid to do this? So many they've killed, even toddlers…"

Tony, Lily, Marcie, Saúl chime in with memories. How he used to turn up the volume on the stereo when "The Ditty" by Paper Boy would come on. And he loved that song, "*Un indio quiere llorar* [An Indian Wants to Cry]," a *quebradita* number by Banda Machos about a poor Mexican Indian who falls in love with an upper-class woman and the predictable result. About how he'd scoop up the younger kids, spin them around.

Tony's father Roberto, a hardworking Mexican man with old-world values recalls Husky with fondness. "Husky's death affected me a lot. It changed me. I stopped drinking—for the kids. We've got to try to understand our children more." He recalls an old Mexican saying: "*Hasta despues de ahogado el niño tapan el hoyo.* [Only after the child drowns do they cover up the well.] I can't let any more of my children drown."

GYPSY

I met Gypsy two years after Husky's death. Unlike some of the others whose photographs are in this book, he seemed to have outgrown his love affair with the death of the "life." We met at an old-style Mexican seafood place in Evergreen. When I arrived, Gypsy was standing on a ladder, poking his head through the ceiling, electrical wires dangling all about him. He snipped at the black and white cords, working a freelance job in his time off from his regular electrician's job, which pays $11 an hour—enough to support the family, his wife, and three kids (7, 4, and 2 years old), and his parents, who all live in the same house.

"I used to straight out gangbang," Gypsy says, taking a break from the job and drinking a beer with a few Evergreen homeboys. "Then I had my first kid and slowed down." He got a job as a utility man at the Montebello Sheriff's Department, but was fired. Around that time MCF ("Michigan City Force," a rival gang) and Evergreen were going at it, Gypsy says, and he carried a gun with him at all times. One day he was driving on the Pomona freeway with his wife and children. A car pulled alongside and some gang-members flipped him off, then tried to ram his car into the median. "I brought out the gun…" He provided few further details, except to say his wife and kids weren't hurt—and that he was sent to prison after the incident. Upon his release, he got a job as an electrician's assistant, and is now a full-fledged electrician.

Gypsy remembers the day his wife told him she was pregnant. He was 17, she was 18. "It was a shock. I thought I'd fucked my life up." He had been working at Sears, but they laid him off—how would he support a family? "I got back on my feet loading

7-Up onto the distributor trucks." Another child a couple of years later. And another. Jobs. Unemployment. "Beefs" with rival gangs. But somehow, he'd kept it together.

Gypsy's is an old Evergreen family. His children mark the fourth generation to live in the neighborhood. Gypsy's grandfather fought in Iwo Jima. A great uncle was on the *USS Arizona* in Pearl Harbor. Three of his uncles went to Korea. A couple of cousins fought in the Gulf War. "They didn't take me," he says with a bit of wounded pride. "Don't worry," says his homeboy Eric, a survivor of several violent encounters himself. "You're fighting a war right here in Evergreen."

After a couple of more beers and stories, Gypsy went home— and the minute he entered his mother and father were on him: "Where have you been? Your boss has been calling! Call! Right NOW!" Gypsy responded meekly, head bowed: "Yes, okay." Mom and dad left for a doctor's appointment, leaving Gypsy alone with his kids, who played rambunctiously on the living room carpet, inspired by the Tasmanian Devil cartoon on the afternoon tube. Above the TV set stood Little League team photos and trophies. "I coached for three years" said Gypsy. "Then they told me I couldn't anymore because of my felony."

He's wavered back and forth across the thin line of barrio life for years. He's buried his homeboys Husky, Gyro, Pablo, and "Little Oscar." But he thinks he's on the right side now. "I've tried to do good and not let the alcohol and the drugs take over." Still, the pull of the neighborhood can be as inevitable as gravity: the weekend before, there had been a shooting incident. It happened as it always does: one moment everything was peaceful, the Evergreen home-boys passing the time on the porch. A car drove by. A hail of bullets; luckily, no one was hit. It was too dark to see who it had been.

Gypsy's response was lackadaisical. "Probably just some young punks who don't know better," he said. Four, five years ago, he would have found out who was responsible—there's always a way to find out—and perhaps organized a "mission" for retribution. But, Gypsy said, "I'm older now."

He dreams of Mexico sometimes. Of packing up the family, leaving the neighborhood and its endless cycle of paybacks behind them. Mexico. He'll probably never make it down there, he knows. But maybe there's enough of Mexico right here, in this house, within this family. Enough love and guidance, enough wherewithal and hope, enough of an embrace for the kids.

"It's an endless battle," Gypsy said. "But you can't give up."

He noticed that his oldest son had scampered out the front door. "¡Mijo!" Gypsy called out. "My son! Where are you?"

Silence.

"¡MIJO!"

Then came the sound of sneakers on cement. "Right here, *Papá*," said John Robert Aguirre, Jr., Gypsy—John Robert—Aguirre's oldest son, poking his head through the front door.

"Don't be staying out there too long," Gypsy told him. "And don't go too far."

JOE RODRIGUEZ'S EASTSIDE STORIES

From 1986 to 1993, I was a writer and editor at the *L.A. Weekly* magazine. Crack cocaine was ravaging the inner city and the war between the Crips and the Bloods in South Central L.A. was at its peak; the gangs had become a major media topic. Writers and photographers from all over the world cruised the streets of L.A. to get the war stories.

Freelance photographers showed up regularly with their portfolios. The images were always the same: gangmembers flashing signs, showing off tattoos, posing with their handguns and assault rifles. These photographers were well versed in the parachuting brand of journalism: drop into the barrio for a day or two, snap the pictures, and get the hell out before you get yourself killed. They didn't stay around long enough to get the rest of the story: that there is often a home the kids return to every night; that for every gang kid, there are brothers, sisters, aunts, uncles, parents, grandparents, godparents who won't turn their backs on children who are both perpetrators and victims of the violence.

When I arrived at the *Weekly*, I was promptly asked by my editor to write about gangs. I refused, arguing that the media's focus on barrio violence severely distorted the picture of the barrio, and that there was much more to Latino life than gangs. The only articles I wrote on the topic during those years were about specific barrio issues: police abuse, black-brown racial tensions, graffiti.

Latino media sources follow a similar path. L.A.'s *La Opinión*, the country's biggest and oldest surviving Spanish-language daily— and by most accounts a fervent defender of Latino causes—rarely deals with gang issues. The few U.S. Latino magazines in circulation put the likes of Daisy Fuentes and Jimmy Smits on their covers, not tattoo-scarred homeboys with Uzis—they won't even touch hemp-gangsta' rappers like Cypress Hill, which features

Latino members. It's a kind of political correctness: don't talk about the dirty laundry, don't give the media powers-that-be ammunition to reinforce the stereotype.

I told myself, and my editors, that I wanted to write about the whole community. But in fact I wasn't writing about the "whole" precisely because I was avoiding the gangs, an undeniable reality— and an issue where culture, economics, and politics collide. In my desire to present a "positive" image, I and other Latino writers unwittingly contributed to the isolation of the barrio whose best interests we supposedly had at heart.

Joe Rodríguez ignored these pieties. He spent over two years shooting practically full-time in the Marianna, Evergreen and Florencia neighborhoods, in addition to documenting a black family in Watts shortly after the riots of April 1992. Since returning to New York, he has made several follow-up trips. He isn't just a simple documentarian: he is a participant-observer, a friend to a great many of the people he photographed.

"The homeboys really called the shots," he says. "I only photographed what they told me I could."

Joe was familiar with street culture: he grew up in Brooklyn, living the vibrancy and violence of his own multi-ethnic neighborhood. He did not arrive at photography until his thirties, after surviving his own encounters with the life and death of the streets. In his first collection, *Spanish Harlem* (D.A.P./National Museum of American Art, 1995), Joe revealed an eye as unflinching as it was sympathetic to the subjects he photographed—from junkies to grandmothers. He can best be described, perhaps, as a Catholic photographer, drawn by empathy to places ruled by suffering, sin, and redemption, places where the most human of impulses commingle with the most inhuman.

As he tells it, he'd had in mind a book on Los Angeles gangs ever since running across a 1950s *Esquire* photo-essay by Bruce Davidson (with text by Norman Mailer) on a Brooklyn youth gang—shot in the very neighborhood where Joe grew up in the sixties. He found the work "warm and lyrical," in contrast to the increasing reactionary hype about the Wild One-like teenagers of the era.

Noting the "savage" images of gangbangers in today's TV news, he set out to find the rest of the modern gang story and capture it on film.

His reception in L.A. was anything but warm. Shot by photographers and camera crews, studied by sociologists, the eternal subject of political (both conservative and liberal) grandstanding, gangmembers are not just reticent about cooperating in such projects; they are often hostile. On more than one occasion, Joe was singled out as a police informant by suspicious gangmembers. And, in contrast to the immediate intimacy he found on the streets and stoops of Spanish Harlem, he found an East L.A. of "houses with lawns and fences" standing in between him and his subjects. But he persisted with his thematic mantra of "families, families, families," and eventually gained the trust of many homeboys and their relatives. He came to such intimate terms with the homeboys that they gave him a nickname: "Joe Kodak." He shared their happiest moments, their most boring moments, their most anguished moments. The result is a photographic journal that in the end is not just about gangs, but also about families, about relationships, about life and death, about fatalism and the possibility of transformation in the barrio.

One night, some weeks after retracing Joe's footsteps in Marianna and Evergreen, I spread several of his photographs out on the living room floor of my house in Los Angeles. I suppose I was wondering about his perspective—the eye behind the camera. As my own eye went from homeboy on the street to homeboy at home, from gang portrait to family portrait, a strange sensation came over me, as if I felt a presence behind the camera: it wasn't just the photographer's. For the images in this book aren't really from Joe's "objective" point of view. One senses a subject behind the lens as well as in front of it, someone intimately related to the kids and their families. And I felt as though I was seeing the neighborhood through a mother's eyes. Joe Rodríguez's photographs tell me that these homeboys are our children: American children, living American lives, in an American city. This point of view—the figure at the center of barrio life—is a mother who'd gladly sacrifice herself to ensure her sons' safety

The idea of family is at the center of many of Joe's photographs. The mother doting over her gangmember sons. The gangmember cradling his own newborn baby. Even in the classic formal portraits of the gangs—flashing their signs, proudly displaying their weapons—we have another family image, that of blood brothers.

The family portrait that stands out most in my mind is of Chivo's family. Daniel "Chivo" Cortéz is a homeboy in his young twenties from Evergreen.

Looking at the photograph, we're in the living room with Chivo, his girlfriend, and their daughter. Various weapons and bullets are scattered about on the carpet. Chivo leans over his daughter, placing a gun in her tiny hands. The terrifying irony in the image is that the poses of all three—mom's gushy smile, the daughter's bewildered wide eyes, Chivo's fatherly concentration—are straight out of a *LIFE* magazine-style series on the quintessential American nuclear family, circa 1954. Which is exactly what this picture tells us. The terror of the streets invades the most sacred of American spaces: the home. The violence of the inner city strikes into the heart of the American family.

Joe fretted over whether to publish this particular photograph; he says he even had nightmares about it. Would the image serve only to reinforce the media's demonization of the barrio? Would the viewer immediately condemn the parents, and clamor for the Department of Children's Services to take the baby into protective custody? Would the viewer suspend judgment long enough to consider it a portrait of the typical, modern American family? (Aren't all Americans, after all, either consumers or perpetrators of violence?)

This photo was taken during a time when paranoia reigned in Evergreen. About a month before, Chivo had been playing with his son Joshua in his car parked in front of the house. A car pulled alongside and Chivo saw a gun emerge from the passenger's window. He instinctively covered his son as a rival gangmember blasted away and then sped off; both Chivo and son were unhurt. The night before Joe took the photo, another incident: a carload of rival gangmembers sprayed Chivo's house with bullets. Again, no one was hurt. But Chivo was certain they'd return. He called up several Evergreen homeboys. That night and the next—when Joe showed up with his camera—they were on watch till dawn.

My gut reaction to the photo was to want to tell Chivo he'd gone mad for placing a gun in his daughter's hands. But the story does not end that night, nor, in this book, with that image. We meet Chivo again at home, sitting morosely at the kitchen table as he gets lectured by his mom—who works twelve-hour shifts driving an MTA bus—to get a straight job. We see him mowing the lawn, and then moments later as he takes a break from the task, lost in thought as he talks to Joe about how he

never came to terms with the death of his father. Later, he's tallying up money from a carjacking, then offering a homegirl a line of cocaine. Now fast-forward, to a mild-mannered Chivo dispatching drivers at the trucking company where he now works, the perfect picture of an office professional. And, finally: Chivo clowning with his son Joshua in the same living room where the first harrowing portrait was taken, this time without the weapons and bullets.

And so we come away with two images: the baby-with-gun picture next to a photo of Chivo displaying all the love in the world for his son. Two possibilities, two futures pulling at Chivo and his family in opposite directions.

Through Joe's photographic series, we have come to know Chivo in all his contradictions, in his most generous and most volatile moments. We *must* know Chivo in all his complexity; if we'd never seen him cradling his kid, we'd never have thought him capable of redemption. We would have written him off as another "Born to Lose" gangmember; we would have never considered him one of "our" kids, just another media monster to beat into submission, to be locked away for eternity.

Chivo is our son. And maybe, just maybe, we can talk to him. Perhaps more importantly—and this, I think, will be the enduring value of these photographs—we cannot just "look" at him, but see him as Joe Rodríguez has seen him: a young man with a past, and the future before him. Just the way a mother would see him. It is a story we need to understand. For Chivo's is not just an Eastside story. It is an American story.

My interest in going to L.A. began in early 1992. I was strongly influenced by the music coming out of Los Angeles and other inner cities across the country. I felt these kids had something very important to say in their music. It was good research. Coming out of the streets of New York myself, I felt connected in some sense. I wanted to speak about things in my work I was familiar with. I was not going into L.A. as a journalist, but as a photographer needing to make connections, and taking the time to get to know people. I was tired of seeing the news covering gangs as animals. I discussed this with the editors I worked with at the time: if you want to break down prejudice in people's minds, it is important to show these kids with some respect, even if they have done grievous crimes.

People always ask me to explain in one or two words why kids join gangs. They want quick answers to explain any image they see. They don't know what the life of a gang member is like; one picture alone can be misleading.

I wanted LIFE magazine to do a photo essay that would show the life of people in East L.A. The photo editor got the story accepted, but in the end they offered to run only a single picture—Chivo showing his daughter how to hold a gun (page 3). I had to decide whether I could accept that. I stayed up nights over this picture. I worried that the image, alone and totally out of context (Chivo, a member of Barrio Evergreen, had been targeted the night before by a rival gang and had stayed up all night to defend his home and his family), would feed into the stereotypes people had about gangs. I asked a lot of journalist friends what they thought. The Brady Bill on handgun control was also being debated at the time in Congress. I decided that maybe it would speak to that issue, and in some way would do more good than harm.

Viewed by itself, it is a very disturbing image. In context, it is less so for reasons the viewer can judge. It is important to note that Chivo has made his way out of gang life (see Carmilla Floyd's interview with Chivo on page 165). I hope this book can provide a deeper understanding of this image, and how it fits into the scenes and stories I documented in East L.A.

—Joseph Rodríguez, January 1998

July 4, '92

When I arrived in South Central, the remains of the riot still lay everywhere, even though it had been cleaned up some. Expecting to find violence, I found a truce between the Crips and the Bloods—families coming together after years of shooting at each other over colors. However, at the other end of town, in East L.A., the truce was non-existent among the Chicano gangs. Ten days after I arrived, I photographed a five-year-old boy and his grandmother who had been hit by AK-47 fire through their living room wall, and a two year old who was killed because a family member wanted to leave his gang. This was difficult for me, having two four-year-old girls at the time myself. Life seemed cheap. Many of the gang members' families I spoke with felt they had been forgotten, no different than the Watts riots of 1965. Forgotten promises.

Post-riot South Central

Casa del Mexicano, Boyle Heights

May 27, '92

At the Community Youth Gang Services—my first contact arriving in L.A.—I was just sitting there waiting for someone to talk to me, and thought maybe I don't have to show faces: maybe wheelchairs, scars, photos of the dead. It is so hard getting access. How can I expose gang culture? I was thinking about details like tattoos, cars and rooms. But that's not the way.

The journals are a way of keeping my sanity; they're extended captions, and a way to go through the process and keep from going crazy while I'm waiting; I have some feeling of the day progressing.

December 1, '92

Large parts of L.A. are Latino. Everybody thinks South Central is predominantly African American, but it's actually half Latino.

L.A. Latinos have a conservative reserve, a Mexican macho reserve; they're concerned about how they appear. The reserve is constant the whole time; the kids won't open up. They'll only let you come so far. They'll say "Don't take my picture in [this or that situation]." It's less so with the younger ones, but it's literally a fucking battle. I have to be comfortable taking the pictures; I want to do more portraits, but there's very few one-on-one opportunities.

Members of Barrio Evergreen gang, Boyle Heights

Evergreen Park, Boyle Heights

Porky and Pony from Marianna Maravilla gang, East Los Angeles

May 30, '93

Somebody told me something very interesting: that Mexicans have more of an Indian philosophy; Indian culture doesn't acknowledge change as much as it respects perseverance. So you're respected if you hang out. It's the same way the kids take bullets; they complain but don't cry. And it's the way I got their respect for taking photos—perseverance —hanging out in the kitchen....

I talked to two sisters who were not happy at home; between them they had one kid and one on the way. I asked them, "Why don't you get out? I know you're Catholic and don't believe in birth control, but now that you are pregnant, what about an abortion?" They replied, "Blood is thicker than water; we don't do that. We're Mexican." They're 22-year-old kids still living at home.

Quiles family, East Los Angeles

Mike Estrada holds a photo of his father who is in prison. Boyle Heights

Member of Eastside Bishops gang
with his son, Watts

O.G.s (original gangsters), Watts

Watts

Roth Eldridge, an O.G. from the Bloods gang, and his son Jacques, Watts

July 4, '92

Gangs seem to start as unstructured groups of children who desire the same as any young group: respect, a sense of belonging, protection. In a lot of ways, it's no different than the boy scouts.

May 30, '92

Jacques Eldridge, seventeen years old, is the son of Roth, an O.G. (original gangster) from the Bloods. He says, "The Bloods and Crips give kids something to identify with, to belong to a pack. It's a substitution for what our people should be giving to them, what the family and society should be giving them. I would feel guilty if I brought a child into the world; there's some serious things in this neighborhood."

I asked him what the gang meant to him: "It's about self-confidence. A gang is a band together of what you feel is your own kind. I think about it like my family. I'm not going to kill for some address or zip code, I'm going to kill for a cause."

May 29, '92

In Watts, choppers pass overhead, acting as back-up for the cops whenever a serious crime goes down. Bobby is introducing me to the Eastside Bishops, telling me to be cool. "Don't be too friendly with them; sometimes a few of the guys are hardcore—two or three percent." They could get smoking the wrong thing, and then all of a sudden I'm the wrong guy, I'm the outsider and could get hurt. I didn't really think about the danger. You don't know how close you can actually get with them. His homies said that I could be black, "Yo! He's from New York." "Hol' up," Bobby says, pulling my coat, "these guys could shoot you in a minute." The choppers pass back overhead, and I get a Vietnam kind of feeling.

Members of Eastside Bishops

Anthony Bolin, five months after being shot in his living room, Watts

Anthony Bolin plays in his living room.

*Member of Eastside Bishops
with his daughter*

South Central

Nation of Islam member sells The Final Call *newspaper. South Central*

May 29, '92

Sherriel Covington, mother and grandmother: "I've been living in this house since 1953. When I was a little girl, Watts was a working-class neighborhood; now the factories have left. Poverty is not a cut and dried issue. I've had an income all my life. When my husband died in 1970, my kids saw I was working my ass off, but wasn't getting anywhere. They would ask, 'why do you have it so hard?' I couldn't explain it to them.

"We don't know how to be parents. My mother felt disappointed that she could no longer take care of us; she lost her dignity. I don't feel sorry for myself. There's so much going for this country. But we need something for the kids—entertainment, community centers, social groups in school."

May 30, '92

There's strong racial polarization among the cops, especially with white cops. It's tough on the streets, and they're not making any progress toward solving the gang problem—just locking them up. The cops' morale is low; budget problems, one cop to a car, the paperwork (they've got files in the trunks of their cars—"Is that the blue or the white form?"—if they don't use the right form in an arrest, they can get sued). The attitude they project on the street is, "Fuck you, I'm doing my job and going home." It's a burnout job.

Member of Eastside Bishops

Marianna members throw their sign. Santa Monica

Quiles family at home: Ramiro and Danny from Marianna, with their mother Aida, and sister María. East Los Angeles

Quiles family at breakfast

Teenager plays with a BB gun. East Los Angeles

December 3 & 4, '92

People aren't opening their doors. It's Friday night. Freezing cold. I'm with Shadow from Happy Valley and his homeboys. They're talking about the wounds of a *vato* who got shot—his liver got turned inside out. They also talk about their prison records. As they start drinking beers and talking, the wind creeps in. Cold. I've gotta kick it with them, but I'm starting to shiver. I can't even take pictures. One takes out his gun, but I'm not allowed to take any photos. This might be a beginning.

June 13, '92

Snoopy from Barrio Street Villains tells me that "joining a gang is like meeting a girl: when you first see her, she's a body until you get to know her. When you get into it, it's about hatred, loyalty and respect."

Porky from Marianna with María

February 26, '93

Last night, Egor was hanging out with the big guys—Frankie, Gyro, Bandit. We all told funny stories about times we got fucked up. These kids are extremely romantic. They listen to oldies, and tell nostalgic stories about the old days. They want to be recognized and to tell their stories—about the dance, about a fight. Gyro will talk about what happened two years ago, when he was shot at a party. That's what they do—just talk about the old days. Two years seems like a long time to these young kids.

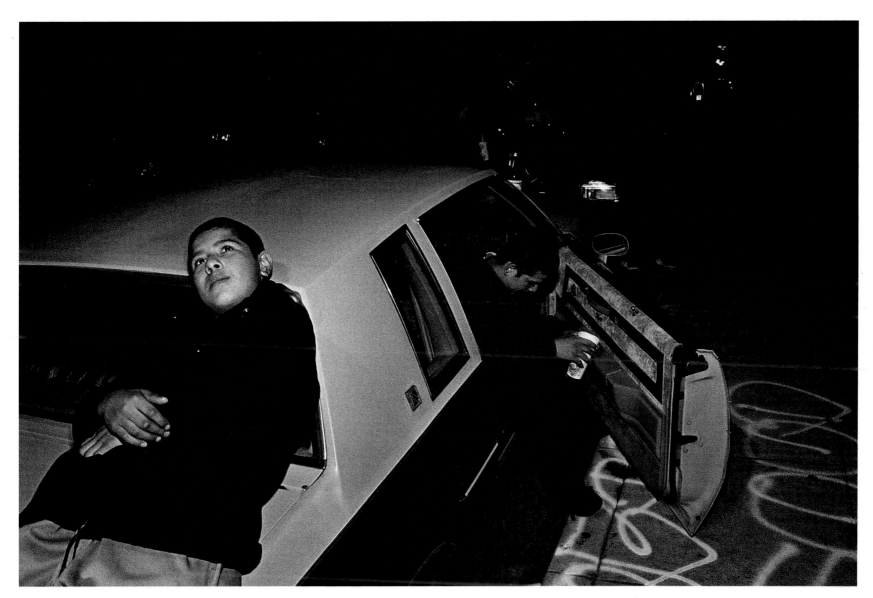

Egor hangs out with Evergreen homeboys.

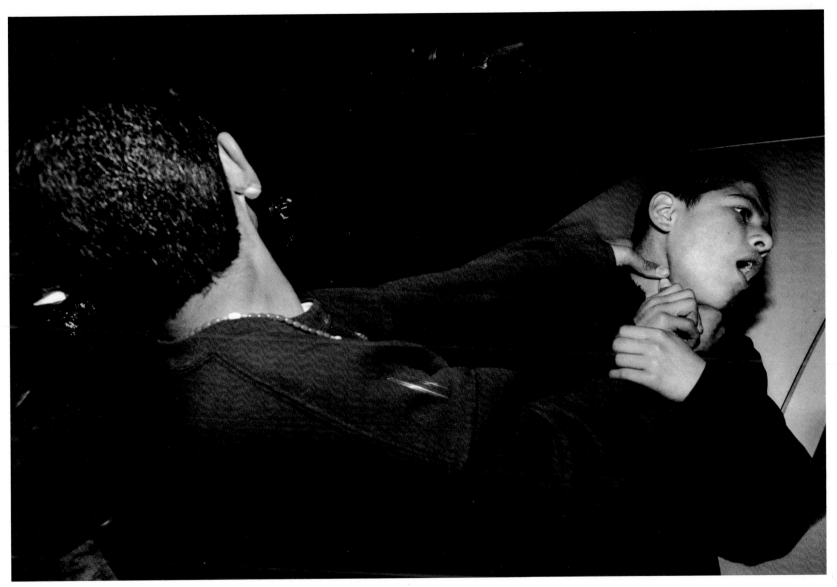

Popeye from Evergreen plays around with Egor.

Boxer, Shy Boy, Penguin, Joker, and Gyro from Evergreen

Friday night at Evergreen

February 20, '93

Gyro talks about gang life with his homeboy Oscar, who's gotten a job outside the 'hood. "I'm glad for you Oscar. I would rather get out; I'm tired of looking over my shoulder. I don't want to die, but I'm down for my barrio."

Tommy and Gyro from Evergreen, with Oscar and Roxanne at Oscar's farewell party

Frankie gives Gyro a haircut, while Spanky plays with a toy gun. They are getting ready to look for a job. Boyle Heights

Frankie and Spanky pay their respects to Gyro, who was killed by a rival gang. Months earlier Gyro had stopped gangbanging.

Herberto Rodríguez's photo album, Fred C. Nelles California Youth Authority, Whittier

June 16, '92

Eighteen-year-old Herberto Rodriguez is lying on a cot in his maximum security cell at the Fred C. Nelles California Youth Authority. This is the third time he's been here. He tells me his story.

"When I was twelve, thirteen years old, I was a wannabe. In my first drive-by at thirteen. I thought it was wrong; I was thinking I might get caught. And then I got locked up for robbery. After that I went to Juvenile Hall for a year and a half for assault. I shot a .380 at fifteen, and was breaking into houses for guns. I was going to school, drinking beer, and shooting.

"In 1990, I went to talk to a girl by my aunt's house. A guy jumped me, and then shot at me. I went into my aunt's house and got a shotgun. Two hours later he came back with his homeboys, yelling 'VIVA EL NORTE;' he was wearing a red rag, so I shot at him. I caught him in the head; from the door I saw the blood running down. I was worried I might get caught. After four weeks I felt good.

" I got five and a half years. Last week I made up my mind: I won't gang bang anymore. When I get out, I want to go straight. They [his gangmembers] know I've been down for the 'hood. When I was jumped in, five homeboys beat me up—I survived the initiation. I have to leave the same way."

Herberto in maximum security at California Youth Authority

June 16, '92

Gang Awareness Class at Fred C. Nelles California Youth Authority. Teacher David Newman asks, "Why are we selling drugs?" One kid answers, "I just wanted to come up, to get things my mom couldn't get me." Newman says that since the riots people are selling more guns than drugs.

February 22, '93

Roman Cisneros is the Dean of Lincoln High School in Lincoln Heights in East L.A. He grew up in the 'hood and went to Lincoln himself. Now he is a formally trained actor; he's appeared on TV and in films. He has taught drama to gang kids at Lincoln, and he's made a documentary about them. "I stay because of the kids. When I'm sitting alone I say to myself, 'when is it going to stop?' I'll try again tomorrow. Because I used to be one of them—welfare, broken home, gangmember—I have to go back and pay my dues. I have to go back where I came from. I don't decide for the kids; they dislike authority. I give them options."

June 12, '92

John Hope Continuation High School, South Central. Almost all the kids come from youth camps. Most of the girls are pregnant. There are twenty in the class, but only twelve show up. Kemo from the Bishops hadn't done any work. He pulls out a folder and eats a hamburger. The girls talk about their hair. Kemo and his friends talk about automatic weapons and how to get one.

The lesson in the class—the teacher is trying hard to keep their attention—is "How did you get your name?" and "What kind of self-image do you want to portray?"

I talked with the teacher afterward: "For all the problems, I believe I can help at least one. Drugs don't seem big with these kids. Out of seventy students about ten will graduate this year. I don't know what we are preparing them for."

Gang awareness class, California Youth Authority

Truce at a gang awareness class, California Youth Authority

John Hope Continuation High School, South Central

Eastside Bishops after school.
A member of another gang throws
his sign in the background. Watts

Largo from Evergreen looks out for rival gangmembers while waiting for the bus after school. Downtown Los Angeles

Community Youth Gang Services counselor talks with Kemo at John Hope Continuation High School. Kemo was later killed. South Central

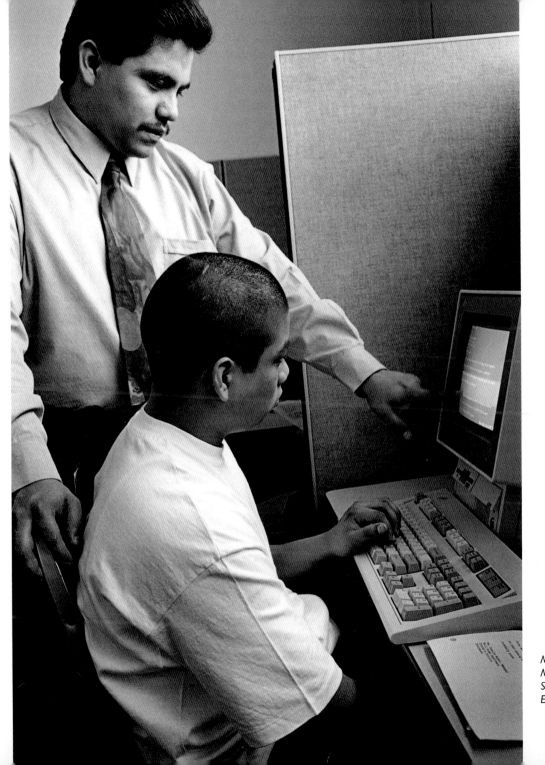

Manuel Garcia teaches César from Marianna in computer class at Soledad Enrichment Action School. East Los Angeles

Dean Cisneros (right) of Lincoln High School questions a student about throwing an orange at his teacher. Lincoln Heights

Evergreen members throw bottles at a rival gang. Boyle Heights

February 25, '93

Cisneros speaks with a young student who is caught with a screwdriver. His mom is sent for, and she comes to the school. He tries to counsel the kid. The kid says his father doesn't love him, and his mother says that his father isn't happy with his job and abuses him. The kid says he's in a gang. Cisneros says these kids are searching for love, needing to belong.

Fred C. Nelles California Youth Authority

Young girl plays marriage. Boyle Heights

Estrada Courts housing projects, East Los Angeles

Gun salesman, East Los Angeles

January 18, '93

Suspicion and mistrust fill the air, fighting against sun and blue skies. After one month I managed to get in with one gang, but only on their terms, trying desperately to get close to their families. I was met with much rejection. After all the studies and stories on gangs in L.A., what difference does one more photographer make? Unfortunately, while in the middle of working with Marianna Maravilla, a few of the members got busted. The sheriff took the photos I had given to some of the kids and tried to use the pictures against them, implicating me in the process. As a result, the gang thought I had set them up—that I was a cop. A setback, obviously.

Exhausted, angry, and frustrated, I tried to move on. I went to another part of East L.A., where after three months I gained the trust of Barrio Evergreen, a two-generation gang started in the '60s. I'm still questioned periodically whether I'm a cop.

Maravilla projects, East Los Angeles

Third Street Sheriff's Station, East Los Angeles

Insane Juvenile Queens, South Central

January 23, '93

El Sereno is on a hill; it's real quiet. I walk up toward the church and get the feeling that it has happened before—that there's been lots of funerals. The funeral is for Thomas Regalado III, a two-and-a-half-year-old toddler killed in a drive-by shooting in front of his El Sereno home. Police think it's gang-related; the boy's 21-one-year-old father thinks that someone came looking for one of his brothers. The kid was riding a Big Wheel behind his fence, and whoever came by sprayed the fence while the uncle was in the back of the house. While the truce between the Bloods and the Crips receives widespread attention, warfare between Latino gangs continues unabated.

During the funeral there was a wedding rehearsal going on in the chapel; they were all dressed up. The coffin was carried in—it was so small. Twenty-five cars drove to the cemetery with a motorcycle escort. I left.

I hooked up later with all the nephews and cousins. It was a Saturday afternoon, and they were all just sitting around, really sad. What do you think happens when a twelve or thirteen year old sees that? The kid must truly be frightened; there's no respect for life. The kids become very passive, throwing up their hands and saying, "That's the way the culture is; it's just part of life here."

June 24, '92

I met a *chola* from South Central. She is now in the Booth Memorial Home for Girls in the lockdown section. She says, "My anger is so bad I don't know what to do with it. I have seen a group of my homies get smoked. I've seen two of my brothers die. I wanted to be a lawyer. How can you turn it around? My mom couldn't help me any more. I was eleven and I lost it. We were all into church then. It's the environment—it ain't about lack of family...for some people. Sometimes I feel discouraged that I joined. I am just going to stay out. I am trying to go to school to get my diploma."

On the other side of town, I meet the Insane Juvenile Queens. It's prom day, and they're joking about all the kids who are dressed up. They tell me about themselves. "It started three or four years ago with the Insane Juvenile Kings; the girls started two years ago. We keep it cool with everyone. We share our secrets, we trust each other; we consider ourselves like family. I don't have sisters, so these are my sisters—Honest, Digit, Sadd, Silk, Grace, Wends, Cash, Sweet, Poor, Bride, and Gem. They are pretty names. We go places together. We never go out alone.

"If I am pregnant, I can talk to the others about it. It's tough for teens here, peer pressure, school.... The news scares people, makes things look bad. We don't want to look like gangsters; killing is not the way. Our parents don't understand. They don't listen to us. They see only the time they were young. When I have kids, I'm going to try and understand them by talking to them."

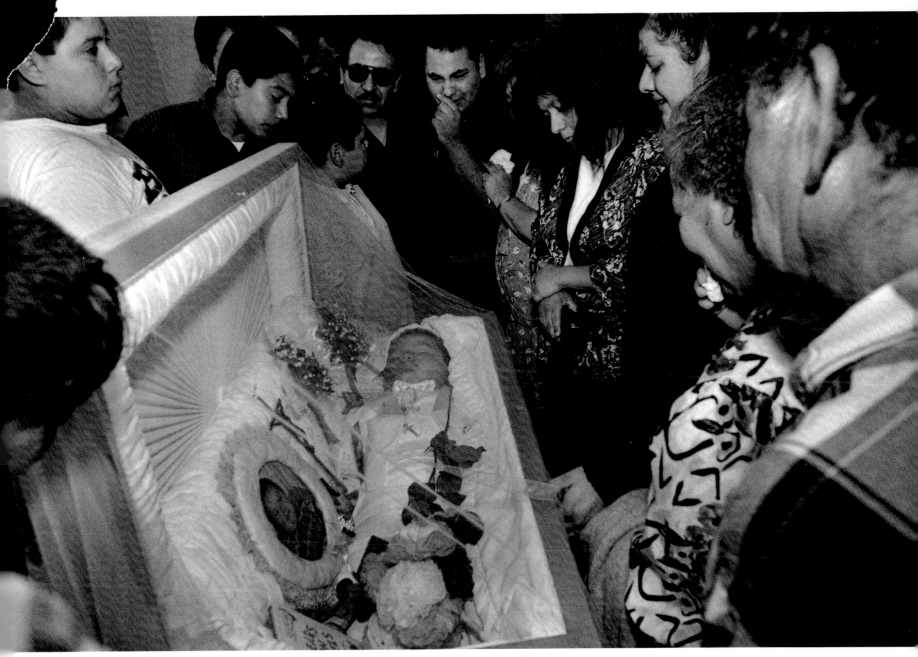

Funeral of two-and-a-half-year-old Thomas Regalado III, East Los Angeles

January 26, '93

I need the strength to persevere…Society has not done a very good job of parenting. Who is responsible? These kids are on a mission to nowhere. They only want to collect stories to tell and drink over—who got busted, what *pinto* (prison) he got sent to. An extremely macho club, where in your twenties you're already considered a *cholo* who's "put in work" (gangbanging: stealing, robbing, shooting at rival gangmembers).

July 4, '92

The photo agency asked for more violence in my pictures. Violence sells magazines. One picture ran today in *The New York Times*: the two and a half year old in the coffin at the funeral. I was really depressed. I can't understand why one must always show violence or famine to be recognized as an accomplished photojournalist. You're always questioning yourself. One of the things you realize is that you are always are missing something; you can't photograph everything. Who am I talking to? It gets hard to gain perspective. Weeks go by and I get these contact sheets (of the previous weeks' work), and they look like shit to me. I know now that I must go back and continue with the families. Have to get closer.

Sheriff's Gang Unit stops gangmembers in their car to check for guns. Carson

Porky from Marianna describes what it is like to get shot.

Popeye from Evergreen checks his .45 automatic before getting dressed for the day.

January 26, '93

Porky, sixteen years old, from Marianna: "I wasn't always a gangbanger. I liked to draw. My mom and dad are *veteranos* (veteran gangmembers, also from Marianna). When I was real young and I started going to school, I was a real loner type. I was heavy, kickin' it all day outside school. One day I started seeing my father dressed up in nice clothes. It was my birthday and I wanted clothes to dress up like that. I wanted to be a *cholo*.

"In seventh grade I got my brainwashing. I saw my friend Jaime ('Pony') hanging out. We started backing up Marianna with the older boys. I didn't tell my father and mother because they would be pissed. I was twelve years old and I had some problems with some guys on my block. Since I was running—chased by the other gangs—Jaime kept telling me to get into the neighborhood. They jumped me in.

"I've put in work for five years. Ford (a rival gang) I hate 'til ever. They shot my mother in the face and my little brother in the hand. They shot at me in front of the house. I have too much heart. I've been through so much I feel old. At fifteen, attempted murder and GTA (grand theft auto), violation of probation, school violation...I have been shot ten times—look at me, I am really limping. I am respected by all my homeboys, wanted by many, hated by others, but respected by all. I love the barrio more than I was loved."

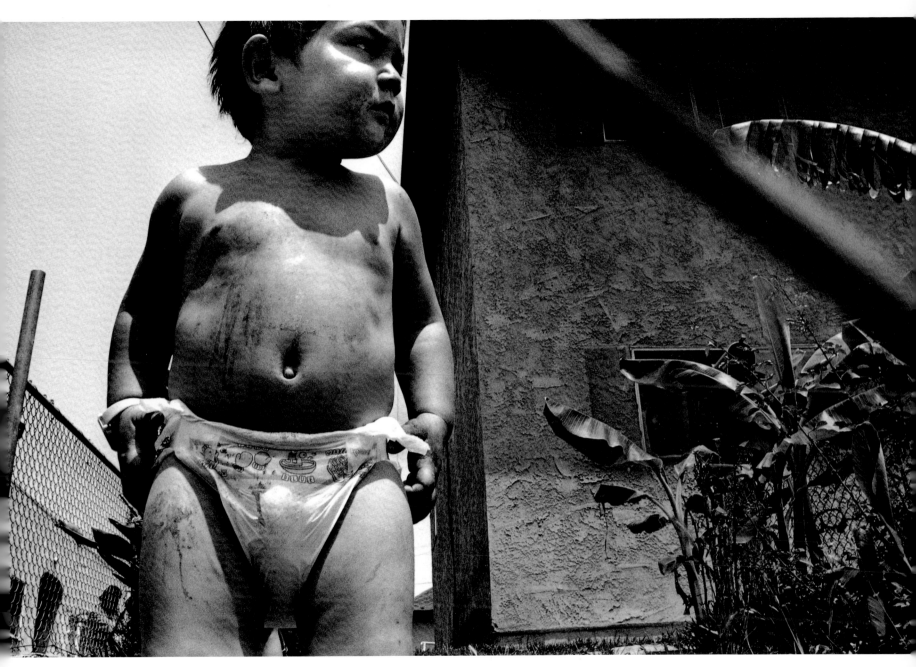

Boyle Heights

Dia de los Muertos [Day of the Dead] rosario [wake] for Husky, slain member of Barrio Evergreen, Boyle Heights

Diablo at Husky's wake. Months later he was killed by a rival gang.

July 17, '93

1:00 AM, Saturday night. César is standing in front of his house, and an Astrovan passes by, going westbound toward Rivera; it turns around and comes back toward them. Chunky, Popeye, and César, walking toward Erik's house, jump behind some bushes. The Astrovan pulls up to Erik's house, next to the bushes. A car door opens; a voice whispers "They're kickin' it right there!" You can hear the bullets scrape against the loading chambers as they fully open the sliding door. They're shooting at Chunky. He pulls a .380. César takes one in the shoulder; he's thrown back into the trees. "There they are; get 'em!" The guys in the Astro pull off about 25 bullets. César, holding himself behind a tree, prays for them to run out of bullets. César gets off three shots—"Hit one," he says. All this takes place within a ten-foot radius. Just another night with Evergreen.

November 1, '93

Dia de Los Muertos (Day of the Dead). At home, Marcy begins to build an altar for her nephew Husky, who was recently slain by a rival gang. Chivo raised money for the funeral. Tonight they will have a *rosario* (wake) for him; family and homeboys start to fill the tiny apartment. It is tradition to honor the dead on this day by bringing all things they had during life: food, clothes, candles, music, flowers, letters, photographs, and cigarettes. Many tears are shed. I ask Marcy what she thinks about the gangs.

"They are always being pushed, by family, society. Jesse (Husky's real name) didn't have a family, although his mom and dad are alive. He wanted to believe in something, but all he found was Evergreen. They build their own prisons in their neighborhoods. It's confusing for a lot of them. Jesse's homeboy Trigger's mom gave him everything, and he says, 'My mom was always too busy.' She would say, 'I have to work.' What Trigger said was 'I would rather have just been loved.' Everyone is trying to prove something. The boy who killed Jesse was no older than fourteen. Before it was kids having kids. Now it's kids killing kids. They have the need for somebody to notice them."

There's twenty people in the small room, mostly Jesse's (Husky's) family. There's tears. Cold air blows through the room, and Marcy says, "I felt him here, I know he was here. Did you feel it Joe?" Gyro comes in and lights a cigarette for him and puts it on the altar. The most emotional scene of all is when Paul, Jesse's ten-year-old nephew, comes in and brings his marbles. Jesse used to play marbles with him. He puts the marbles on the altar; he is really crying.

Husky's tombstone, Resurrection Cemetery, Montebello

Evergreen members at a house party

Husky from Evergreen with a homegirl from another neighborhood

Scoob Dog from Evergreen

May 30, '93

One time I went with them to buy guns. The ease of access in getting them is a joke. We drove into the hills and stopped outside a house. The selection ranged from .22s to AK-47s. We asked for two .380s. $150.00 each. He goes down to his BMW and comes back in twenty minutes. We give him his money and get two brand new .380s. I had thought that all the guns were coming from Mexico, but they were packaged in brand new boxes. The label read "U.S. Gun Co. of America." It was like going to the grocery store.

Each gang will have a certain number of guns, mostly owned by the gang. They're kept stashed and taken out when they sense the need for protection, or for a party to make a show of bravado by shooting at gang rivals' cars or into the air. The younger kids treat them like toys; Husky shot himself in the testicle playing with one. If a gun gets lost, they get another.

February 26, '93

Kickin' it in the neighborhood, meeting all the *vatos*. Still hung over from last night. Today Husky and Bandit try to hustle a fifteen-year-old *chola* from another neighborhood. "I know what you want," she says. "Once you have me then it will be all over the neighborhood."

Members of Florencia 13 gang outside school, South Central

Danny and César from Marianna

Porky, César, and Pony from Marianna

November 24, '93

At the beginning I made a few very powerful images—like the kid with the scar (one bullet in a hail of gunfire pierced five-year-old Anthony Bolin's living room wall, tearing through his stomach, kidney, and lung before exiting his grandmother's elbow; he had been watching TV). There was an openness in that family; it gave me the energy to go further. I found myself becoming more family-driven, focusing on this as a theme.

These days I'm taking less photos; I'm driving people to jobs, taking kids out to eat (some go two days without eating!), helping a seven year old do his homework, even taking some girls to an OB/GYN clinic. I've rushed Trigger to the hospital after a shooting. No pictures are coming out of these encounters. To just photograph the violence doesn't cut it for me. It misses what the story has to say.

Danny Quiles from Marianna

March 14, '93

Barrio Evergreen had a party last night, slappin' high-fives, "Yo! homies!", gang signs bouncing with the music, "Here are the heads—let's jam!", I'm jammin' *vato*. They play around with each other, being macho, like boys do. Mark (Egor) started hanging out with Evergreen when he was eight. Later I meet a *vato* who had just been released from prison—ten years for murder. He says to me, "Just don't make *La Raza* (the neighborhood) look bad."

The most tiring thing is that only a few in Evergreen know what I'm doing; "Joe, what you're trying to do is deep," they say.

Popeye from Evergreen

January 25, '93

Joaquín from Marianna Maravilla tells me: "Being in a gang really limits you to a small area to live in. You can't leave the block. I don't know where to go. I like staying here taking care of this side, so we are always on guard."

Clown and Largo from Evergreen

Brown Faces

Pablo "Diablo" Trujillo

So many lands,
so many different places,
all that I see is the same brown faces.
Day by day is how I live,
ask me why?
That's just the way it is.

So many lands,
so many different places,
all that I see is the same brown faces.
Doing whatever they can to survive,
because we have to stay alive.
We must live long
and make a change.
Oh God give me some strength.

So many lands,
so many different places,
all that I see is the same brown faces.
Killing one another,
is how they survive.
You should see the pride it gives 'em
to see another brown face die.

So many lands,
so many different places,
all that I see is the same brown faces.
At Evergreen Park is where I stand
looking down on the world
as if I was all that.
Standing proud and tall
over the world with nothing to hide.
There's no shame in my game
I'm from Evergreen Gang.

Here they come once again
L.A.P.D. trying to stop my game.
Once again I laugh,
as I see the patrol car pass on by.
They don't want to stop,
They don't want to start no war,
'cause it won't be over
'til one of us hits the floor.
They're too scared,
so they just roll by.
I know they don't want,
a piece of my mind.
I speak with knowledge,
and without fear,
I see nothing to live for here.
I don't care if today I die,
I'll just be another brown face.

Barrio Evergreen gangmembers: (top row) Downer, Largo, Trigger, Popeye, Chivo, Clown; (bottom row) Puente, Bandit, Tweet, Baby, Penguin

March 5, '93

What a night. Tired, sick, but still I go to the Evergreen meeting, only to be cut down by two of the older heads. Scooby said I was cool, but there's so much suspicion in the air you can cut it with a knife. They are definitely a brotherhood. I was told to get out of the meeting; they were talking about the seriousness of drive-by shootings with the younger ones. The older members were explaining how they were "paying for their mistakes"—the younger ones doing graffiti near the park jeopardizes the older ones with drive-bys, etc. It's the constant abuse I take—being shot down like that, and a fifteen year old telling me what to do—"You can't do that."

I take a drive downtown, to look at the tall buildings and cool out. Watch white folk stroll for the evening and kiss on the bridge, amidst the skyscrapers. The distance between East L.A. lowrider hip-hop and the Los Angeles Philharmonic is just crossing the bridge, and you're there. I drive, and everything looks beautiful on this side. Meanwhile, across the bridge the guys were planning sinister madness....

Evergreen members confront a rival gang. Boyle Heights

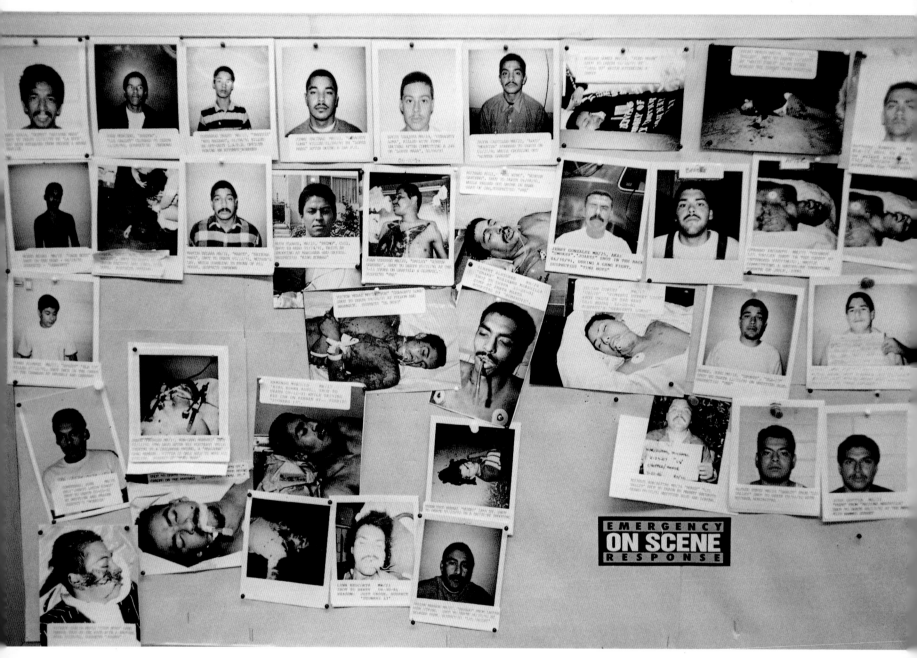

Third Street Station homicide board

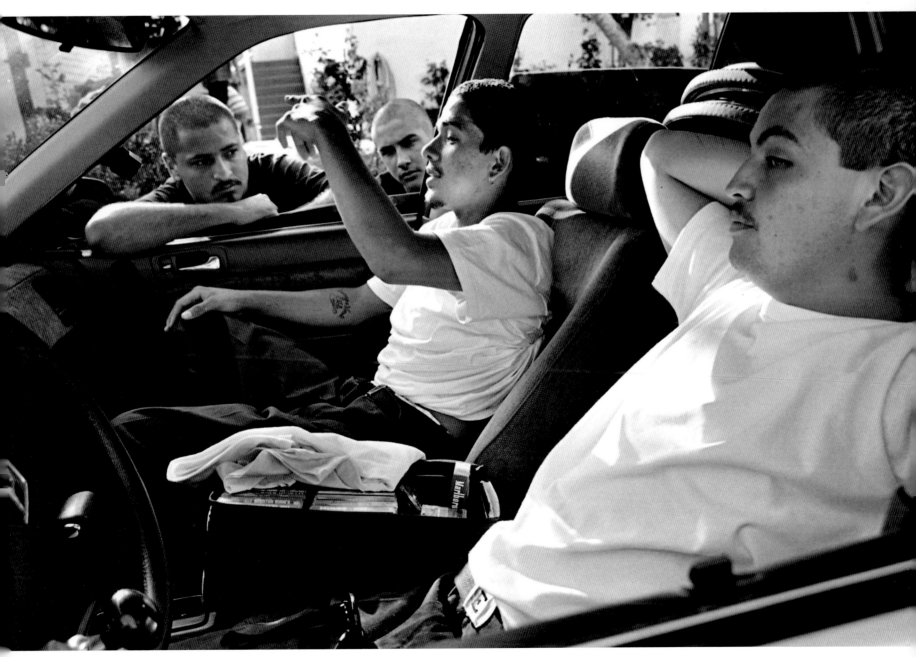

Evergreen members Penguin and Largo talk with Popeye and Tweet (in car). Boyle Heights

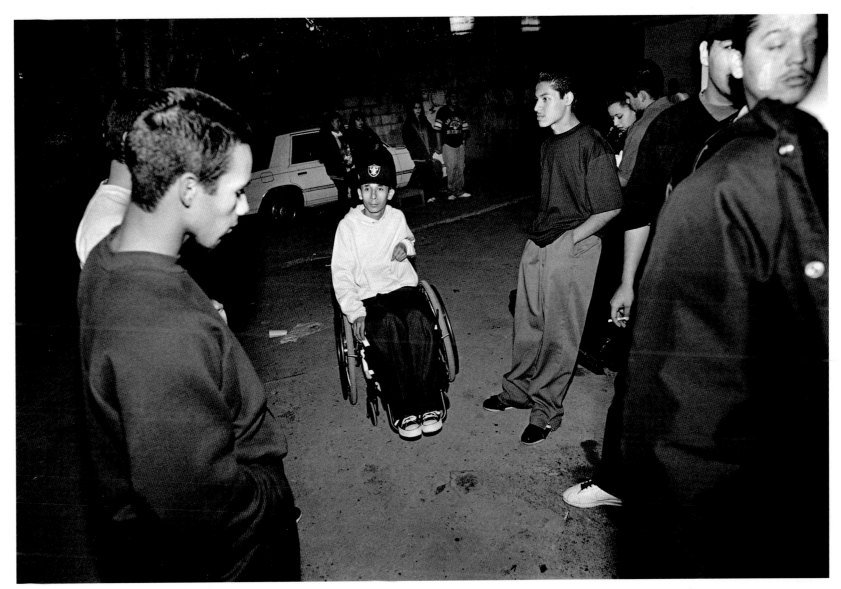

Friday night, Marianna Maravilla gang

Diablo from Evergreen hangs out with Beatrice and her daughter in Evergreen Park.

Danny and César from Marianna

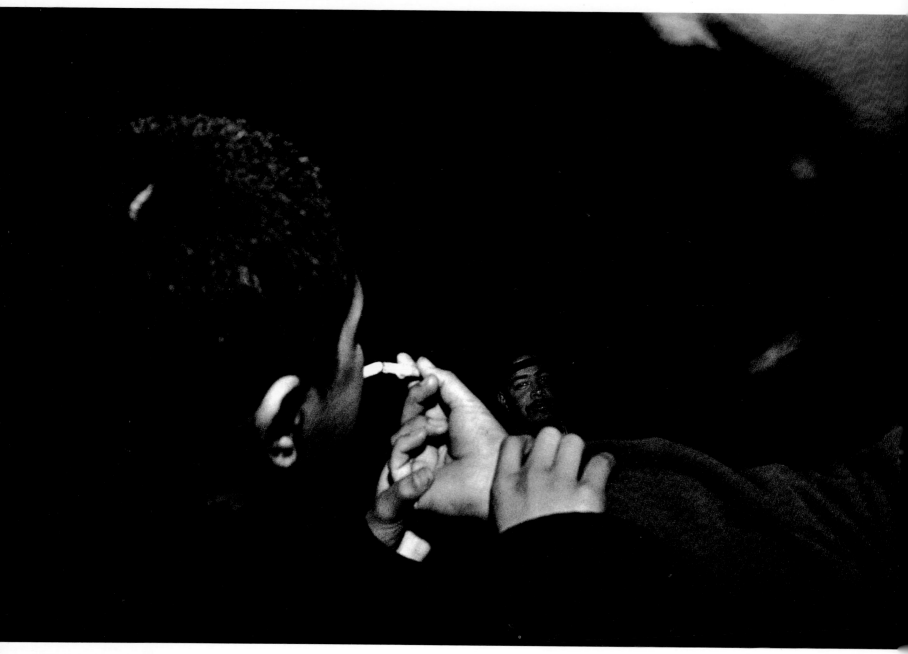

Egor hangs out with Evergreen.

Baby and Largo from Evergreen

June 5, '93

1:30 AM Rivera and First Street. We were kickin' it after the truce meeting. A van parked near by with a girl inside, falling back and laughing. The homeboys followed it to the corner. First Street's a two-way street, and at the corner there were two cars. One car shouted "Fuck Evergreen," and so Evergreen shouted "Fuck you" back, but the second car had guns. One *vato* was shot four times, but he didn't die. The bullets went right by my face.

This changes my relationship with Evergreen. Now they know I'm down for them. "Hey man, did you see Joe? Man, he's crazy—bullets were right there."

The night of a truce in East L.A., seconds after a drive-by shooting, a Clarence gangmember is hit by fire from an automatic weapon. He survived. Boyle Heights

Deputy Fidel Gonzalez holds a confiscated gun at the Sheriff's Property Warehouse. Whittier

April 11, '93

Scooby pulls me up: "Most people don't care about us; why would they want a book about us?"

Silent, Chivo, Scoob Dog, and Penguin from Evergreen show off their hardware.

April 28, '93

Chivo wakes up for breakfast with his mom Ema and sister Andi. Jesse comes over and has coffee with them. Ema talks about how Danny (Chivo) looks like his father. The night before we went through her family albums looking at photos of her when she was younger. We talked about how I had given my mom a hard time. Ema feels she did a lousy job bringing up her kid; "it's difficult for any parent to raise kids in this environment." Chivo says he needs to make money, so he is thinking of dealing herb. Jesse deals. Later we go to Chivo's son's mother's house to give her money, and then we go to Yvonne's (Chivo's daughter's mother's) house to help pay some bills.

May 3, '93

Over the weekend White Fence (a rival gang) shot at Jesse's car—gave him a flat. They also shot at Chivo, who was sitting in front of his house with his son and wife when they drove by. Chivo jumped on his son to cover him. Luckily no one was hurt. Chivo and his son's mother are extremely on edge. No one has slept this weekend. Some of the homeboys came over for support, and all the guns start to come out. Chivo and Jesse feel like their days are numbered. Their parents just throw up their hands; "what can we do at this point? It's all up to God."

Chivo looks out his window for his homeboys. Boyle Heights

March 26, '93

Ema walks through the door after her early morning shift as an RTD (L.A. Mass Transit) bus driver. "I've been driving for eight years." After greeting her son, whom she says she has given up to the Lord, she sits down at the table to open her mail. She is a strong woman of Mexican stock. We talk about her family background, how she was extremely close to her father. He worked for $3.25 an hour and managed to save enough money to buy three houses. But the relationship between the two was shattered when Ema had her first child when she was fifteen years old. Her father stopped talking to her. "He lost all respect for me," she says. "I have seen so much…I am so tired. I have been the strong one in my family. Being alone is not easy, raising the kids in this city." Chivo just sits and listens. Later we decide to go to a restaurant, but Chivo says he can't eat there because it's in his enemy's territory.

Chivo with his mother Ema, sister, and friend Boxer

Chivo mows the lawn.

March 16, '93

Chivo's mowing the lawn; "otherwise my mom will get on my case. I need a job." He's nineteen going on twenty. "I never did heroin and I stopped smoking weed. My father used to slam (do dope), and I seen what what my mother went through. I used to deal, but stopped. Didn't like what it did to people."

He tells me that he holds a lot of anger. "Youngsters are growing up with more hatred and anger than before. Seven years ago when gangs were coming around, it was rare for them to have two or three guns—they were just for the heads. Now they all have to have guns. They don't give a fuck. I wish we didn't have to wear guns, but in these streets it's necessary."

"When my dad passed away—I used to go to my dad when I was in trouble—he was in his forties. Cirrhosis of the liver. August 28, 1989. Still to this day it hasn't hit me. I didn't shed a tear; my heart didn't want to accept it.

"All my life I was going back and forth between my mom's and dad's house. I guess I'm still wanting to go back to my dad's house. I know if my dad were alive I wouldn't be a *cholo*; I'd probably be a houser, listening to music and hanging out with girls."

Chivo counts his money the morning after a carjacking.

Chivo turns a homegirl on to cocaine.

Chivo at an Evergreen house party

March 17, '93

Chivo at home. Went to the market, cashed a check, played two lottery tickets (got our money back), and went back to his house. He and Gyro and a few other heads went to this factory in East L.A. advertising for jobs, but all they got was "We'll call you." Nobody wants to hire a gangster.

Chivo, his son Joshua, and sister at home

Chivo at work as a truck dispatcher, East Los Angeles

Interview with
Daniel "Chivo" Cortez

YOU'RE NOT BANGING ANYMORE, WHY IS THAT?

I got a job now. Work changes everything, it really does. When your mind is focused on something else, you don't have time or energy for banging. You find that you don't have time to hang out in the neighborhood. You work, you come home—you're tired, you wanna relax, be with your family.

You ask all the guys, "What will change you?" and they'll say, "Give me a job. I'll change." And you know what? It does. They will. I'm a perfect example. One out of ten, maybe, they like the lifestyle of the drugs and the gangs and all that. But, within a year, you're going to that person's funeral. A job changes your life.

But it's hard for a gangmember to find a job or to even get an interview. Or if you look like a gangmember—if you have the baggy clothes, the shaved head—it's hard to get anywhere. There are a lot of people who're prejudiced. If my uncle hadn't worked in the company where I got a job, they wouldn't have given me nothing. They would've given me one look and turned me away. Bald heads, nowadays, it's weird: if a cop sees a bald head, boom, he's there, his eyes are on you, he's checking you out, checking your car, checking who's in the car with you.

HOW EASY IS IT TO GET OUT, TO CHANGE YOUR LIFE?

Well, it's not easy. People are still after me. There are still a lot of places I can't go because of who I am and where I'm from. I still carry a gun. I think I will always have a gun, because of the way people are now, especially out here.

I did move out of East L.A. once. One summer, I was fighting fires with the Forest Service in West Covina. But I felt out of place. The way people stare at you, they have so many prejudices. That's how I felt over there; I didn't feel comfortable so I came back. It's weird. Life's crazy. They made me change. Now I'm prejudiced against them—white, black. When I come back here, where I grew up, with my own people around me I feel safe…I feel at home here because I don't feel like somebody's looking at me because I'm brown, like I'm a sore thumb.

That's why I moved back here to Evergreen. I mean, first I moved away from here 'cause I had problems in the neighborhood. Then they killed one of my friends, Ramiro ["Gyro"]. After they killed him, they saw me and said, "Hey, he's the closest one we can fuck with so let's fuck with him." That house where you came to see me last year got shot up and so did the car. We were all in the house. Me and the kid and Yvonne. We all hit the floor.

They said they killed Ramiro by accident—they thought he was somebody else. I believe it, because there are a lot of stupid people who just wanna prove a point. Especially if there are like six guys, and someone says, "That's the guy!" and the others go: "Yeah, yeah!" And if that guy has a gun he's gonna want to prove himself to them, he's gonna act like he's somebody. That's when mistakes happen. That is how innocent people get killed. I never really felt like I had to prove myself, except maybe when I was younger. But it was never just to anybody. It was to somebody that hurt someone I knew, like my homeboys.

So I'm not saying it's easy. It's hard. There are still times, even at work, when people talk down to me. Someone said something about a restaurant, and someone else said, "Are you crazy, they don't have those down in East L.A. It would be all tagged down and graffitied down." It makes me mad. East L.A.'s always been portrayed like that. As violent. You know, it's like when I see stuff on the news about Bosnia, and I'm sure there must be places in Bosnia where people are friendly and life is pretty normal. Because it's not where you live or where you're at, it's who you are. It's crazy. They just pick up on what that little crowd does and blow it up and people go: "Oh, Bosnia, let's not go there."

Just like East L.A. My boss at work, he asks me, "Why don't you move out of there?" I say, "Hey, you make it sound easy. Why don't you give me the money, give me a raise, and I'll do anything you want me to do, man." But I wasn't brought up in the lifestyle you were. You can't just say get up and go out.

• • •

In a different way, I kind of like it [the bad reputation]. Like when people at work ask me where I live and I say, "I live in East L.A." They go: "You do? Oh shit. Do you hear gunshots and stuff?" And I just say, "Sure but you just gotta stay inside. When you go outside, just go to your car and mind your own business, don't go out and check who's shooting." Or sometimes, when I tell them, "Hey, I couldn't sleep last night 'cause of the gunshots and helicopters and shit," and they get all panicky. And to them it's like, wow! And they feel intimidated.

I used to be really particular about my clothes for that same reason. I used to iron my clothes for hours to look good, to impress and intimidate. I'd wear my gang-affiliated wear—my white T-shirt, Ben Davis, and Nikes—so people would know, "Hey, there's trouble walking down the street right there." They'd know I was from somewhere.

How did you get into the gangs?

When I got into it, I was about 13. My dad was one of the reasons. I'm not blaming him or anything, but he passed away right at the time when I got into my teenage years. Before that, every time when I would get in trouble at school or anything, my mom would send me to my dad. I think there were a lot of times that I got into trouble later in life because I wanted to be sent to my dad. But then there was nowhere my mom could send me 'cause he was gone. My mom would get so angry, she'd just tell me to leave the house. I missed him a lot. I still do. It hasn't really hit me to this day, that he's gone, I feel like he's still there. When I hear people saying bad things about their fathers and mothers, I wanna tell them, "Hey, I lost my father. You only have one— one father, one mother."

It started just hanging out with friends I grew up with. Everybody at that age, they try to hang out with who they think is the in-crowd. All it takes is just one person, to get you involved, to get you introduced. It was fun when we were just hanging out. But after a while, it started getting more violent. A group would have a name, a street name. Suddenly, you're part of a gang—you're part of that one crowd. At 13 or 14, I'd be around guys who were 21 to 22. Gypsy and me, they would give us beer and treat us like men, you know. I think that's a big part of why kids get into these things. It was for me and for some people I know. We felt we were treated like adults. It felt good to be treated with respect. You feel like a family—it means a great deal. Since I didn't have it with my father, and my mother didn't know what I wanted…

Out in the streets, you get treated equal—you're getting treated the way you want to be treated. By the time I was 15, I was screwing around, deep into the gangs. My mom knew what I was doing and used to keep me inside all the time. I used to feel like I was locked up. I'd say, "Hey, I'm not in jail." I know now she did it to protect me, but she never told me that. I think that's what people need to be told. "I don't want you to get hurt, I don't want you to get mixed up with the wrong people." I know I'm gonna be different with my kids. You gotta learn from your parents' mistakes.

■ ■ ■

But that's how it happens. And now, it's happening all over again. Like, this is Second Street. There are fifteen young guys hanging out on that corner down there. They call themselves the Second Street Boys. It's like an egg hatching. Later on, it's going to get worse. Somebody's gonna take maybe one of their bikes or something. Then they're gonna back up each other, and from there on it's gonna get worse and worse. Someone's gonna have a knife and another one's gonna have a gun. Then it's: "Hey, they've got a gun. Well, that's alright, let's get three or four guns. Hey, let's get ten. Let's go back over there and get them." Back and forth. Back and forth.

I can see it happening right in front of my eyes. You see all these kids just hanging out, doing nothing. And it's hard to know if it's them, if they're just rebellious, or if it's their parents who don't care. I know how I used to be. And you know whatever you tell them, they're not going to listen. Nowadays you can't say, "You can't do this and that because this and that is gonna happen"—they don't know. They haven't been through all that shit. They don't think about it. All you can tell 'em is, "Hey, be careful, man." What you know from experience. Like: "Hey, be careful when you see these cars coming at night. If you see a lowrider coming up with music and you see a bunch of heads in there, be careful. They could be out looking for somebody or something. Look to see if the windows are up or down. Look to see what kind of object comes out of the window. Is it a gun or a bottle? Are they going to throw something?" I'm telling them because I already know.

SOME PEOPLE SAY THAT GANGS AREN'T BEING STOPPED BECAUSE THE "ESTABLISHMENT" WOULD RATHER SEE YOU GUYS KILL EACH OTHER OFF AND SAVE THEM THE MONEY AND EFFORT.
I don't really think they want us to really kill each other but…they just don't want anybody from down here going up. To me, I'm not really into politics, but I think a lot of the things they do are stupid. Like Pete Wilson, that's a guy who's prejudiced with power. Like the three-strikes law, that's real stupid. A guy steals some cigarettes, that's one felony. Then he does another petty theft, another felony. Then he steals a pizza from some kids, and they give him life. I mean, literally, his whole life. Then, on the other hand, you have some guy who turns around and kills somebody—they only give him twenty-five years. This other guy just stole materialistic things, and they give him life. That is so stupid.

Prison don't solve anything. It just makes you smarter in crime, that's all it does. You're in there with a bunch of people who've got knowledge and tell you stories. You come out, you're filled with all this bad knowledge. Nothing good about that. I've been in prison. I've been accused of murder, been in there for three murders. I was never convicted, though. I was in jail for little things also, but murder was the main thing. I was scared, all three times. I thought that was it. If you're behind bars and think you're gonna spend the rest of your life there, damn, you're scared then.

If I hadn't changed I'd be in jail or dead. Or if I was out, I'd be selling drugs and making money. Or trying to make money. I was never into taking drugs myself. I was always more into making money. But now, that's where the job comes in. I have money now, so, I try to do with my kids what my parents never did with me, and that I wanted to do. Now for instance, two weeks ago I took my kids to the circus, "Ringling Brothers, Barnum and Bailey." You heard about them? I took my kids and spent about $150. It felt good. I was happy to see them happy. I took all four of them. That was the first time I've ever been to the circus. First time. It was good. When they come back, I'm gonna be the first one to buy a ticket. If my kids don't wanna go, I'll go alone!

I try to do things with all of them that I've never done. The kids are what really give my life meaning. That's another reason I don't wanna jeopardize nothing. If I go out now and mess up and go to prison, I'm gonna lose my job. If I lose my job, I lose my money. If I lose my money, I can't keep anyone happy. Then I'll be miserable and I'll be pissed off and then I'll go straight back into the 'hood. I'll carry my gun, be pissed at everybody and pissed at the world. That's how I used to be. Pissed at the world, didn't give a shit about nobody. People would try to tell me, "You gotta do this, you gotta do that," I'd say, "Fuck that. I can get it faster, I can get it quicker, I can take it." If I wanted it I could take it. That's what I used to do. If I had a car like yours and I wanted to fix mine up, I'd take yours. If your car had a nice system and rims, I'd sell it and I'd get money and buy something that I wanted.

What I'm doing right now is trying to forget my past. You have to try to avoid thinking about the bad things, because if you think about them you'll get the nightmares again. I'm trying to start something new. I have a job now, I'm trying to be responsible, which I give myself credit for. I got my license back, I work hard. I'm trying to give it my best. It's not really like I want to forget all my past. If a friend comes to me and says, "Hey, I need help," I'll try to help him the best I can. But if he comes to me and says, "Hey, some guys did something to me, and I need you to do a ride, man, let's go shoot 'em up or let's do this and that"—that's something I really will not do right now.

DO YOU FEEL OLDER THAN 22?

Take somebody that's about 30 or 40 years old, with an average lifestyle, say someone who lives in Anaheim or any average city, I bet you I've been through more tragedies and more hell than they've ever heard about or seen in their life. Or gonna see. The only violence they see is in movies or in the news. I grew up with that. I've been through more things than they've ever seen. It makes you harder. Makes you meaner. It does.

Interview conducted in August 1995, by Carmilla Floyd, writer and editor-in-chief of the Swedish youth magazine *Ocean*.

For an update on Chivo's story, go to http://www.powerHouseBooks.com/East_Side_Stories/Chivo.html

Egor's sister, Yvonne Olvera, Evergreen Park

LA VIDA LOCA: Joseph Rodríguez and Luis J. Rodríguez on "The Crazy Life"

JOSEPH RODRIGUEZ:

So what do you think about the future of gangs? Are they just going to proliferate? Are they going to die off?

LUIS J. RODRIGUEZ:

Gangs can't die off until the foundations for them die off. They're going to continue as long as we have these kinds of conditions that we're living in. Kids are really looking at gangs as the only intense, integral experience they can find—the only structure that gives their lives meaning. As long as that's the situation they're going to go into gangs. I keep thinking that I can get kids into something else. But many keep getting further into it, because they need it. They need the gang. So I'm not here to attack gangs. I know why they exist. And what I would like to do is to start getting young people to want to be in a service for life, not in a service for death. There are two ways to be a hero, right? They want to be heroes, these kids. They're willing to die in a

blaze of glory. They want to die in a fight, it's a heroic thing. [But] heroes can also want to live because their life has meaning and purpose, and not want to just die or kill somebody because that's what society is telling people to do.

J. R.:

One of the things I wanted to ask you about is the origin of the gang icon of the happy and sad masks, commonly associated with the masks of the theater—comedy and tragedy. You mentioned that the association of these symbols with gangs goes way back. Can you go into some of this history?

L. R.:

It relates to something that I think goes back to pachuco times. The pachucos were the first generation of kids from the Mexican Revolution. The Mexican Revolution brought a million immigrants into the U.S.—a million more died in the revolution, so you had this great upheaval.

J. R.:

Brought in?

L. R.:

After the U.S. conquest of the Southwest in 1848 and the discovery of gold in 1849, the Mexican population was thrown off of their lands.

So, you didn't have that many Mexicans in California by the turn of the century. Then in 1910, the Mexican Revolution started, and all of a sudden you had all these refugees coming over. They would set up their own little shacks, and that's how the first barrios started.

J. R.:

Like *colonias* [colonies—poor, Mexican makeshift neighborhoods, still found in the south of Texas]?

L. R.:

That's right. They were all *colonias*. And then one or two generations later you had estranged youth who weren't

175

part of the American culture and they weren't part of the Mexican culture. They were constantly beaten up on. So they created their own culture.

The pachucos were the epitome of rebellious youth. El Paso was where they started, but L.A. made them a monster culture. One thing about the pachucos is they did things that most kids hadn't done before, what a lot of kids do now: they had strange clothing, a new way of talking, in Spanish or English, they tattooed themselves all over. They had a walk, you know, they had a style. The closest thing to them, I guess, was whatever was coming out of the East Coast with the African American and Puerto Rican communities. They shared certain things like zoot suits, but the pachucos were really alienated youth. I think they served as a model for all of the 50s rebels, the Hell's Angels and the punks. These youth were completely pushed aside in the culture, and so they created their own.

But, also it was like a spider in a web. They were caught. They were entangled. They could not leave the world they were in. They had good times and they had bad times. It was like you couldn't change it. It was this super-fatalistic thing. And I think that when the youth were really rebellious,

the system moved against them. They were imprisoned at a higher rate than other people and they were beaten up during the so-called Zoot Suit riots in the 1940s. Heroin was also brought into the pachuco community in the 1940s, I'm convinced on purpose.

It happened in all the major areas, where young people fought back— black, brown, white. But if you were a pachuco, you were caught. You couldn't leave it. And in many ways, that's what this "smile now/cry later" thing is: "This is your lot, man." Right now, you have a good time, and some day you're gonna pay. It's always like you're gonna pay for whatever happens. If you have a good time, when it's over, you're gonna get it on the other end.

You start feeling like nothing really good can happen in your life. Everything seems trapped inside a web. You can't escape it. I guess that's why the *vatos* [dudes or guys] would tattoo that image of the spider web all the time. Ultimately, your lot was to never really go beyond *la vida loca*, "the crazy life." The prison walls were the end of it, you know.

J. R.:

You have a national perspective on gangs from your work and your traveling. Tell me what's going on in

Chicago. How is it different from L.A. in terms of gangs?

L. R.:

I think the similarity is that L.A. and Chicago are the two largest industrial cities in the U.S. Factories, steel mills, rubber plants, and meat-packing— all these things created the kind of economy that families and communities depended on, and an awful lot of these factories have closed down. There's a lot of displacement. What you're seeing in both L.A. and Chicago is the largest rise of gang violence we've ever seen. And that really makes sense because you have all this economic displacement. In that way these cities are similar.

I think the main difference between the two cities is that the history of L.A. gangs goes back farther. The barrios in L.A. are the oldest continuous street gangs in the country. We have several generations. Chicago also has multi-generational gangs, which began later in the late 40s, but mostly in the 50s. In Chicago, where you also have a large Latino population—Puerto Rican, Mexican—you have gangs like the Latin Kings and Spanish Cobras. These are gangs that have been around for awhile, but in Chicago they tend to emulate the African

American gang structures. In L.A., it's really the Chicano, you know, the *cholo* experience that even the Bloods and Crips emulate. They give their props to that style. Almost everybody in L.A.—whether you're talking to Asian kids, or white kids, or black kids, or Salvadoran kids, whatever they are—gravitates to the *cholo* culture in one form or the other. They add to it or take away from it, because it's the culture that best speaks to their anger, their rage.

It turns out that the intensity of the Latino gangs per capita is worse than with the African American gangs in the United States. Although, in sheer numbers, there are more African Americans in gangs. These kids look at the gangs as the only way they can deal with the crisis that's going on in their lives—not having any options. Prisons are becoming a rite of passage for them. I'm fighting the same thing in Chicago as in L.A.

J. R.:

Let me interject here. I caught an article on the front page of the Sunday *New York Times*. It was a big story about the homicide rate, and how it has gone down in many large U.S. cities, especially those with minority populations. Do you see this as a sign that gang violence is easing in the long term?

L. R.:

Let me tell you: statistics cannot tell the whole story. But one thing you can get from statistics is that the media has exaggerated the problem. Let me give you an example—and I don't want to put down any death, because, you know, every death is important. In L.A. in '92, there were, I think, 800 kids in the county who were killed in gang-related shootings. In Chicago there were 140 gang-related killings, which is a big difference. Hey, 140 is a lot of kids, there shouldn't be one, right? But the police claim there were fifty thousand gang kids—

J. R.:

In Chicago?

L. R.:

Yeah. So if you take 140 killings out of fifty thousand gang kids you realize that most of these kids aren't killing anyone.

J. R.:

Right. The media plays it up.

L. R.:

It's getting overblown. It's bad enough that some of these kids are dying. That's happening and it needs to be dealt with. I think a lot of this is because all these guns are coming into our community from the outside. And that seems to be the only way that people can deal with problems. But it's also true that most gang kids are not killer kids. Most of what they do—90 percent of what they do—is hang out.

J. R.:

Now that you bring that up, there's no doubt about it. I spent three years hanging out with gangs here in L.A. There is this big fallacy that people think gang life must be all about shooting people. You know, it is 90 percent boredom. I mean, I was just as bored as they were because all we did was just hang out. But then, every once in a while, there was that one moment when a drive-by happened and someone got shot.

L. R.:

There's nothing to do out there on the streets, nowhere to go. It is boring. Most of the time is waiting—"What are we going to do?" That's how it is in these streets. Most kids are just trying to find something to do, and there really is nothing. They just want to meet girls, meet guys. They just want to do what any kid wants to do. But our kids are demonized or glorified. Either way it's the wrong way of looking at it.

This is part of a larger problem, an economic one. I mean, this whole economy thrives on the fact that there are people kept idle so there will be others who need to work for almost nothing to keep their families alive.

J. R.:

Especially now, more than any time in recent history. I mean with all the layoffs.

L. R.:

The deeper reason it is going on now is because of this transition in our economy. The last time we went through this was when our agriculturally-based society was industrialized. Now it's the industrial-based society into electronics. If we understand that, then we know that this is not unexpected—it's got to happen this way. The difference is we're in a different time now. This is a whole new world. This is what's causing the revolutionary movement we're seeing today.

But, you know what, the power is in our hands. Latinos, African Americans, poor white people, we've got the possibility of bringing that technology to bear toward our interests. We've got the possibility of having abundance really coming toward where we are. We're at a crossroads. But if we

allow these Republicans and some of those Democrats to get away with prison-building instead of economic development, then we're all going to be behind bars! I mean, we're all going to get caught up in it.

But, if we look at the possibilities, then our goal should be to realize those possibilities. This electronic age, this technology, can be a liberating thing.

J. R.:

So I gather you feel like this is a very important time in history right now?

L. R.:

I think it's one of those great moments in history. You know in these transitional times, it can go either way. We either go with it, or we go against it and pay a big price. At every step, with these changes that we've talked about, we have the choice to destroy our opportunities or to advance them. I think we have a chance to advance. But, if we're not careful, and we don't understand what's happening, we could lose it all.

J. R.:

How does one pull oneself up? I can share my experience, but you, for instance, you sure went crazy—the crazy *vato* that you were back then. You know, running around and hanging out

and getting high and all that. How did you find your way out? Or was it luck?

L. R.:

It was a combination of things. One was that we were in the late 60s, early 70s, and those were the movement days. You had the Black Panthers, the Brown Berets, the Young Lords, the American Indian Movement.

J. R.:

A political awareness?

L. R.:

Political activity was happening. You notice that if you looked at those neighborhoods at that time, gang violence was at its lowest point.

J. R.:

Also, affirmative action had just begun, right?

L. R.:

Yeah, well, people were getting into it. You had the Economic Opportunity Program. Some of the homeboys were becoming college students. They had *pinto* [ex-convict] programs where they'd take guys from prisons into universities. It was an opening, a small opening in which people were getting knowledge, buying some options, gathering some resources, and coming back to the 'hood and looking for people like me. It was a highly political time. I was taught by revolutionaries.

The Chicano Movement had different aspects to it. It wasn't a monolith. Some people just wanted to be in the system; some wanted to make money; some really wanted to make changes for the people. I got into the most radical, revolutionary section of the movement. And you know why I thought that was important? I needed it. I needed that intensity.

You can't take a gangmember and then suddenly tell him to join the boy's club. If you've been in that intense life, *la vida loca*, you need something just as intense. And what these revolutionaries did was to turn me on to a lot of reading and a lot of knowledge. They had me read books, study hard. They encouraged me to get out there—get out into the street, talk to people. There was a whole community of revolutionaries that surrounded me so I wouldn't go back into the heroin; so I wouldn't go back into the gangbanging; so I wouldn't go back into jail. And it helped. It worked for me. It didn't work for all the people we were trying to attract, but it worked for me.

J. R.:

I agree with you. I was also strung out on heroin in the late 60s, early 70s. But I was also politically aware. The Young Lords were happening in New York; the Black Panthers were active; the Weathermen and such. And I was also against the Vietnam War. That gave me a sense of identifying with something. Something of wider consciousness, not just the ordinary Hollywood version of what to identity with. I had to look at my life and where it was going: it wasn't going anywhere. I mean, you know, just going from Riker's Island, out in the street, dealing drugs, coming back, doing this and that.

There were opportunities then, definite opportunities. I remember first getting my GED in an old factory building, taking classes at night. I was on the methadone program then and decided to do something with myself because I was really down.

But, one of the great things to happen, for me—besides meeting a couple of people who helped along the way—was the camera became a new way to look at life again. At that point images sparked something in me. I was this kid who grew up not being able to communicate. It felt like I was learning to do that for the first time. I learned

how to express myself, to show what I saw, and how I saw it. I didn't change right away; it was a slow process. But, the opportunities that were available then, for education and job training, helped turn my life around.

I think that what happens with photography, with the picture process, is it's a way for me to express myself. And for people to notice that I'm alive. And also to notice that other people are alive. We all need to be seen. We *have* to be seen.

L. R.:

What you are bringing up about your experience with photography is important. It's important to see that getting into art at some level is also healing. It's transcendent. I got into writing and poetry. I even did murals. But here, you found it through the camera, a place where you could transcend all these experiences and put it into an art form. And to me this is the experience a lot of these *morros* [little homies] and some of the *rukitas* [young women] need to have. They need to have that kind of an expressive art form where they can work out some of the things they're going through. Without it, how can they move away from the madness? They're too caught up in it.

J. R.:

Absolutely. It's harder today, though. There were programs then helped me. I went back and took this college adapter program that prepared me for college. We studied Shakespeare and Baldwin—poetry and poets, and writers that I would not have run across otherwise. Something definitely changed my life there. And then right after that, I got back into school and slowly got off the methadone program and, boom. Tuition was cheaper then. There were some grants. They even gave you some car fare to go to school. No big deal, but enough to get by with.

I think educational opportunity helped get me out. Which brings me to the question: how do we educate our kids? I'm very concerned about this now. You know, coming from that "me" generation, or that old *tecato* [heroin addict] way, that old drug habit way of "me, me, me." Now, I have two children of my own. I look at a lot of the kids that I photograph in the United States and I think about where we are headed. Where are we headed in terms of the future and trying to have something positive going on for these kids? We have people coming out of really good universities right now who can't get jobs, right? So then we talk about turning against one another. Our government's great at turning groups against each other because then they're not taking the blame.

I know it's complex, but do you think kids can still be helped if they come from a bad environment but are still getting a sense of something really interesting in school, something they can identify with? Do you think that might help?

L. R.:

I think it could. The problem is that schools seem to be caught up in things, like devaluing kids right off the bat. Schools should be the place where you are encouraged to get creatively and intellectually engaged. I don't care where you're coming from, or where you are. Once you do that, all the kids will win. You know, it doesn't matter if you're poor, if you're on welfare, or if you've got a rich family. If you're at a school that says, "We see you all as capable of all these great things. Here's all the resources. If you make mistakes, cool. We'll keep trying." That, I think, is what these kids need, and that's what we've got to give them.

The public debate keeps coming back to why aren't we getting our lives together? Why aren't we picking ourselves up by the bootstraps? But nobody works harder than inner-city poor people. Nobody spends more time trying to get their families together than they do. And still we can't make it—I see the problem as systemic, it's not just about individuals.

J. R.:

Explain that for me a little more.

L. R.:

I'll give you an example: I went to Bryn Mawr, Pennsylvania; I did a poetry residency at five schools there—all private schools. Parents pay $17,000 a year for their kids to go to those schools. Almost 90 percent were white kids. There were some black kids, some Asian, some Puerto Rican kids, but most were white.

Great kids, lovely kids. I had no problem with these kids. They were creative. They were expressive. Their art was all over the walls, and they were learning. They had a 100 percent graduation rate and a 100 percent college entrance rate. And I'm wondering, "What's the difference? Are they better than you and me? Are they better than our kids are?" The difference is that they are not allowed to fail. Nobody will let them fail—even when they want to fail, even when some of them are suicidal. Some of those kids are on drugs. Some of them are alcoholics. They've got problems like anybody. But, man, they put resources behind them so that they will make it. Our kids don't have these kind of resources.

You know, the only time anybody ever got up and said, "Why don't you inner-city people pick yourselves up by your own bootstraps?" was at one of those Bryn Mawr schools. Some kid, a white kid with glasses—a smart kid. He thought he was making it because of his own efforts, and we poor folk weren't making it because we weren't willing to work at it.

J. R.:

That's interesting, so did you talk to him?

L. R.:

It was kind of odd, but he didn't realize that all his life someone's *taken care* of him. He didn't even think about this. He thought that it was all his doing.

J. R.:

In your travels, going across the country, do you ever bring up the issue of whether people from well-off communities are willing to pay more to support the rebuilding of this society? I mean, it's a big issue—everything's about money in our country. And if we

want to get some things done, we need to put more money into it. When you look at a country like Sweden, where I lived for a couple years, things work there because the tax revenue is very high. Money does go into certain things. Here, are we willing to pay higher taxes to make people's lives better?

L. R.:

The cutting off of their community from our community is so great that they actually think that we're not the same community. My thing is these are all your children. They can't see this because supporting brown and black children—even poor white kids—seems like paying for somebody else's. But they're paying for *our* kids, for our community, for our city. They are American kids. And they look at them like they're from another planet. And so they say, "Why should I give you money?"

I say, "You're not giving me money. I'm paying taxes, too. That money goes into your pocket. My taxes pay the subsidy that keeps some of these schools in some of those communities going." But they don't want to pay for programs because they're for "other" people. And that's where all that distancing and relocation has really destroyed our ability as a culture to

come together. The ones reaching out are getting slapped. The separation is deep. I've talked to communities where they feel some sense of compassion, but as soon as you talk about inner-city youth, their compassion stops.

Kids suffer. They go through so much pain. We have to think about how to turn that around. How have we been reaching those kids who are completely abandoned—they don't know where to go. How do we get them back to touch something that's invaluable—that creativity, that imagination which is inexhaustible. Creativity, that's what keeps you persisting. Sometimes I think I don't have any more to give. Then I go back in there, and hey, there's more—more art, more energy, more words. You're always creating. That to me is the power that we have as human beings.

Look at the South Bronx, where they created this language art from nothing. Kids that were thrown out of schools, into the basements with turntables. Poetry coming out of kids; art on the walls. This comes from something deep. Something intrinsic to human beings. You push them down and then they come back at you from another end. And that's the resiliency of the human spirit—that's what gives me hope.

J. R.:

You're an established writer now. How do you get up in the morning and, you know, get out there and keep the hope going? How do you, Luis Rodríguez, keep the faith? I mean, I know some days I get up and I go out and try to make pictures, and, sometimes, I feel like I can't make it. How do you keep it going? Can you speak about commitment?

L. R.:

Well, it's really hard sometimes. I'll tell you something: I just had a light-weight heart attack.

The heart attack was a warning. I thank God that He didn't take it away from me right there. He let me have a warning sign to think about what I want to do. To me, it's important to have a purpose in life.

J. R.:

I also wake up and say "Jesus, what am I doing here?" You know? 'Cause I've got a whole other agenda that I have to struggle to deal with now. You become a professional. You have to try to get the work out. I have to deal with the magazine world. That's where I make my money.

Editors see these twenty or thirty pictures of the gang story. And, of course, some are going to take the most graphic images and put together a sensationalized version they want to publish. I feel there's a real strong sense of compromise in my work. In order to get it out there—to publish—I have to be able to take my work and shape it into what editors want. It's tough not being able to tell the whole story, the whole truth.

But it's like you said—it's important to just keep it going. It's a struggle. And like you, there's a lot of anger in me, which comes out through the camera. But the anger can be channeled in a positive way in terms of trying to get close and listen to people. I think we have a very big responsibility. And I know that there are people who will want to hear this voice.

I could be abroad documenting the conflicts in Bosnia or Sudan, but, you know, within our communities, that's where the war is. Right here in the streets of America. That's something I want to address. It's something that's from the heart. There aren't too many people who are going back and working in the barrios.

L. R.:

You have a responsibility. We're not like artists who are hiding in their studios or their lofts. They're doing their art for themselves and they don't care what anyone thinks. We have a responsibility to the voices of the people who can't speak. For the homies who died. I know I had somebody—more than one person—get mad, 'cause they felt that I was selling out because Simon & Schuster/Touchstone Books published my book. Hey, you know what? They're buying into me, man. I'm not buying into them—they're giving me the means so that I can get these voices out. That's really what's driving us.

J. R.:

That's the truth.

L. R.:

That's opening up avenues and doors—so kids can get this book. Kids in jails, kids in schools, kids in the inner city, kids in the heartland.

Always Running, La Vida Loca: Gang Days in L.A. was written to explain, to touch anybody who's ever been through that. I feel that what I have to do is to give knowledge to people, to network with people, to hook them up to whatever organizational ties exist that can help people make it in the world. The idea is to encourage other people to tell their story.

J. R.:

But these kids, they come up to you and they've read your book. What are they telling you? Do you see a ray of hope in their eyes? Do you see them wanting to become writers?

L. R.:

I see what I felt when Piri Thomas's *Down These Mean Streets* got into my hands. I was 16 years old. I couldn't relate to people. It was like looking at Piri Thomas and saying, "Hey, that's me, man." He was in Spanish Harlem. I was in East L.A. But it was a lot of the same. We were going through the same thing. We need that. These kids need to know that their lives are important. That they're valid. And then they need to know that there's a path *out* of what they've been through. That's the job we have to do. A lot of these kids feel that they're stuck. They feel like that gang motto "smile now/cry later." The spider's web. They tell me—as sometimes I used to say—"This is the way it's always been, this is the way it's always going to be." If it's the way it's always been, so it must be the way it's got to be. Nothing can change. My book is giving people the idea that, "You know what? He went through it, went through all this non-sense, and he did change." It's possible. There's a pathway now for them.

J. R.:

I agree. To me, another key is the support of family. What do we do to keep the family alive and strong? That's a tough one, no?

L. R.:

It is, but you know, somehow in spite of all this, families have continued to be there. And you know, you can't really have a good family when it's not economically viable to have one. That's why all of these families are failing. Still, there can be exceptions. You know, even when I look at mothers, raising these kids without fathers, I see them doing a beautiful job. I think that the idea of the nuclear family is overrated. I've seen sisters raising kids with no mother or father. And I see them do a beautiful job. I've seen fathers, just single fathers, raise good kids. Love is the key.

But I'll tell you something else. A family can't do it in a vacuum. As long as one kid is at risk, they're all at risk. And so in my struggle to be a father, I also have to struggle for my community, so the community can help raise these kids, too, and can help give them guidance. This means that I have to love my children, to care for them and protect them; I'll do my end of it. But the community needs to come in and say,

"Okay, we'll give you alternatives, we'll give you direction, we'll give you some options. We'll give you mentoring. We'll give you people who will come and take you somewhere. Give you some artistic development." You know these kind of things we just don't have now. How can you be a good father or a good mother when the rest of the community has abdicated its responsibility? It hurts all of us.

J. R.:

How do you see your role as a parent and as a gang survivor?

L. R.:

I'm very fortunate. It is what gives me a lot of responsibility, too. I think about the ones who have gone to the grave, some of the guys. They were better people than me, man. It's the luck of the bullet. You know, when you're in the wrong place, wrong time, good people go down.

I'm one of the survivors. I figure, okay, I wasn't one of the best people. But you know I've got to do the most with it; I got to carry it for the ones who didn't make it. I've got to try to speak as honorably, as intelligently, but also as responsibly as I can for them. I don't want to misuse what I think has been given to me. I have to be honest. And I think it's important for all of us to learn that. We speak for a lot of people. I figure this is what I have to do. This is my cause.

I have these youth I'm working with. And my own kids. They give me something to live for, fighting for a world with them. Not just for them but for all young people. I go to the juvenile facilities and it brings tears to my eyes, to see these young men and women locked up. And they're crying to me.

I'll give you an example. The last time I went to a juvenile facility—I think it was in Santa Cruz—I went in there and had some good talks with the kids. They took me to the lockdown section, to the really hard-core kids. And they were all in their own little cells. They had these huge, thick walls with plate glass. I was talking to one kid through the wall. Hey man, the sparkle in his eye—this kid had soul, he had feeling. And he wanted me to read him a poem. So I remember reading right through a slit between the door and the wall. And he had his eyes closed, his ear pressed to the glass. And I'm reading a poem through the door. And that hurts me. This isn't right. But what keeps me going, man, is because I'm so angry. I'm angry. They're trying to put my own kid in prison.

I'm angry because I have children, and I have grandchildren, and I see what they're going to face. I'm angry because everything you do to build a better world for your kids is being undermined by the racism, the economic nonsense, these politicians running around doing what they want to do. That's what keeps me going. And I don't want to die. I mean, twenty-five years ago, I wanted to die so bad, I did everything I could to die. And now, believe me, I don't want to die. I've got a lot of work to do.

J. R.:

I remember when I was young, 15, and I didn't have any wherewithal, or any experience, or anybody to ask. At first I didn't see how it was possible for me to achieve anything of importance.

But that changed, and that's what I want to try to relate to a lot of the kids. That's why I wanted to sit down here with you for this interview to try to tell kids, so they'll know a little bit of who we are. Not just this thing about, well, just another photographer who took some pictures. That we have a sense of struggle, that we have seen some struggle and we're going to see more struggle. I hope they see that it's possible to do things.

You know, I also wanted to emphasize this point to the kids who do get to this book: it's not something that happens right away. It's not something that comes to you in a year, or a month, or six weeks. It takes years.

L. R.:

It's true. When you get older, your perspective on time and struggle is different. Years ago, I was willing to die for very little, man. I wanted to kill for very little—someone made me mad, somebody gave me a dirty look, somebody stepped on my shoes. I determined my life's worth by what I was willing to die or kill for.

But now I'm willing to die for something big, something monster. Things like justice. Peace. This gives my life meaning that's commensurate to what I'm willing to die for. That's why I'm not going to do stupid things. That's why I'm not going to take drugs and drink my life away. I even pay my parking tickets. I make sure that there are no excuses to fail.

J. R.:

You know, it's actually amazing, when you think about it, how much we've changed, from what we used to do and how we did it.

L. R.:

That's what kids don't get a sense of—the long haul. It's not really provided to them very well in our culture.

J. R.:

No, because in our culture everything has got to move so fast.

L. R.:

But I never gave it up. If I did I'd give it up for everybody. Persistence is part of what we have to carry with us. You can't lose the dream. Keep going for that thing way out there. It's not going to be an easy path, man. It goes back and forth, up and down. But I learned one thing: even when you go backwards, when you slip back, you never really go back to the way you were before. You're always advancing. And kids don't know this. Somebody's got to help teach them this, that they're always going forward.

J. R.:

That's it. You know, if somebody said to me, "We don't have any money, but what can you give the kids, what can you teach the kids?" That would be the thing that I would try to teach them. I mean the magic thing that happens with this connection is that, if you find something that you really love, it doesn't become the work issue anymore, it just becomes something that you have to do. You get up, and it's part of your life.

L. R.:

Now we have something that's keeping us going. And to me this means taking care of people who are hungry, taking care of people who don't have homes. To work with people so that they can in fact work for themselves. You know we've got to be *for* each other, and that's the best way to find God. Everything tells me that you don't just find God by yourself, sitting on a corner somewhere and trying to get back at everybody. It's in having to work with people and going through relationships that we need to go through. Finding people who are suffering and being there. You see the face of God in all these children. That's what it's all about.

Interview conducted on August 10, 1995, in Los Angeles.

Boyle Heights

Joseph Rodríguez is a New York-based photographer whose work has appeared in *The New York Times Magazine*, *National Geographic*, *LIFE Magazine*, *The Village Voice*, *Vibe*, *Sí*, *Spin*, and numerous other international publications. Rodríguez's photographs have been exhibited widely at venues including the International Center of Photography and the NYU Tisch School of the Arts, New York, the California Museum of Photography, Riverside, the University Art Museum, Berkeley, the Mexican Museum, San Francisco, and the Fort Worth Museum of Art, Texas; and internationally at the Centro de la Imagen, Mexico City, the Kulturhuset, Stockholm, the Fotograficentrum, Gothenburg, Sweden, and the Festival de la Photo, Arles, France, among others. He is the recipient of several grants and awards including a National Endowment for the Arts Fellowship (1994), the Mother Jones International Fund for Documentary Photography (1993), and an Alicia Patterson Fellowship (1993). His first book *Spanish Harlem* was published in 1995 by the National Museum of American Art, Smithsonian Institution and D.A.P. Rodríguez is represented by the New York photo agency Black Star and the Stockholm-based Mira Bild Arkiv.

𝕽𝖚𝖇é𝖓 𝕸𝖆𝖗𝖙í𝖓𝖊𝖟 is an award-winning journalist, poet, and performer. Currently the Los Angeles Bureau Chief at Pacific News Service, Martínez was formerly the news editor of *L.A. Weekly*. He is also co-host of PBS-affiliate KCET-TV's politics and culture series, "Life and Times," for which he was awarded an Emmy in 1995. He has lectured and performed widely at such venues as the Los Angeles County Museum of Art, the Whitney Museum of American Art, New York, X-Teresa Alternative Art Space, Mexico City, and the University of El Salvador. His work has been published in *The New York Times*, *The Los Angeles Times*, *The Village Voice*, *La Opinión*, and *The Nation*, among others. Martínez is the author of the critically-aclaimed book *The Other Side: Notes from the New L.A., Mexico City and Beyond* (Vintage). He currently resides in Mexico City where he is working on his second book about the changing cultural and political landscape of Mexico for Metropolitan/Holt.

𝕷𝖚í𝖘 𝕵.𝕽𝖔𝖉𝖗í𝖌𝖚𝖊𝖟 is a renowned poet, journalist, and critic, whose essays and poetry have been published in *The Los Angeles Times*, *The Nation*, *L.A. Weekly*, *The Americas Review*, *Poets & Writers*, *The Chicago Reporter*, *Hispanic Link*, and many others. Rodríguez has received numerous awards and fellowships, including The Carl Sandburg Award, a Lannan Foundation Fellowship for poetry, and the 1989 Poetry Center National Book Award of San Francisco State University for his first book *Poems Across the Pavement* (Tía Chucha Press). Rodríguez is the author of the critically acclaimed *Always Running: La Vida Loca, Gang Days in L.A.* (Curbstone Press and Touchstone/Simon & Schuster). He has lectured and performed worldwide, appearing at the Center for Documentary Studies, Duke University, University of Paris VII, PEN World Congress (1989), and Barrio Sandino, Nicaragua. Formerly of Los Angeles, he now resides in Chicago, where he is director of Tía Chucha Press.

EAST SIDE STORIES: Gang Life in East L.A., Photographs by Joseph Rodríguez

Published in the United States by powerHouse Books
a division of powerHouse Cultural Entertainment, Inc.
180 Varick Street, Suite 1302, New York, NY 10014-4606
telephone 212 604 9074, fax 212 366 5247
e-mail: info@powerHouseBooks.com
web site: http://www.powerHouseBooks.com

First edition, 1998

Library of Congress Cataloging-in-Publication Data:

Rodriguez, Joseph.
    East Side stories : gang life in East L.A. / photographs by Joseph
Rodríguez ; essay by Rubén Martínez ; interview with Luis J.
Rodríguez.
        p.   cm.
    ISBN 1-57687-002-2
    1. Gangs—California—East Los Angeles—History. 2. Hispanic
American youth—California—East Los Angeles—History. 3. Hispanic
American youth—California—East Los Angeles—Social conditions.
I. Martínez, Rubén. II. Rodríguez, Luis J., 1954- . III. Title.
HV6439.U7E2257   1996
364. 1'06'60979494—dc20
                              96-21023
                                 CIP

Hardcover ISBN 1-57687-002-2
Limited Edition ISBN 1-57687-003-0

Art Direction: Yuko Uchikawa
Project Coordination 1993-1995: Paula Curtz
Essay Editing 1995: Michael Schwartz
Project Support: Sandy Close, Pacific News Service
Duotone Separations by Rainbow Graphics, Hong Kong
Printed and bound by L.E.G.O./Eurografica, Vicenza

A complete catalog of powerHouse Books and Limited Editions is available upon request; please call, write or visit our web site.

10 9 8 7 6 5 4 3 2 1

Printed and bound in Italy

A slipcased, limited edition of this book with a signed gelatin silver print is available upon inquiry; please contact the publisher.

Illustration on page 49 by Ramón Espinosa. Illustration on page 119 by John Lira, courtesy *Teen Angels* magazine

Book design by Yuko Uchikawa/MAKERS' STUDIO